Be
Gentle
with
Yourself

by

Nisha B.

ISBN: 979-8-218-11049-9

Table of Contents

Acknowledgments

This book is first dedicated to my son and my mother.

I strive to make you guys happy!

Son, you are the best thing that has ever happened to me. My little role dog. You motivate me in ways you will never understand. Everything I do, I do it for you.

Mother you are my very best friend! I love you and you are the best mother ever! I'm so grateful for our bond and I hope it stays like this forever! Travel and shopping buddies for life!

Shout out to my family and closest friends! You know who you are! You guys are truly my village and I need you. I love you and appreciate each and every one of you. You guys don't judge me and are very supportive. Thank you for always being there for me.

Epilogue

What do you see when you look at me? Most people see a beautiful, black woman, a single mom with her head straight on her shoulders, so happy and stress free. How do I know this? It's been said to me several times. People are always asking me how I am so happy. Why am I always smiling and laughing. How do I work full time and take care of my son.

What people don't see is this beautiful, black single mom crying in the middle of the night. Discouraged and overwhelmed because she has to do everything on her own while everyone else appears to have help. What people don't see are my insecurities. That I have a hard time standing up for myself. Letting people talk to me any type of way and having the fear that they will never speak to me again if I express how I feel. What they don't see is the frustration of the single motherhood journey.

I have pain that came from childhood that followed me into adulthood along with added the pressures of being a black mom in America. This life isn't all glitter and gold. It's not all rainbows and bunnies around here. I had to pray hard, study hard and work hard to get to where I am today.

On the bright side, my momma taught me to leave my attitude at the door. I know we all heard that before. So, I leave my pain at the door. *"Save your tears for the pillow"*, as Abby Miller would say. Never let "*them*" see you sweat right? Well, I'm here to tell you I understand. I know the pain, the frustrations, the heartache. I get it. I had to learn how to accept my journey for what it is. Love where you are in your journey because you are exactly where you are supposed to be. I had to learn how to forgive myself and now I want to help you do the same.

I wanted to write this book because life is truly a journey and although we experience bad times we have to remember to thank God for the bad times just as much as we thank him for the good times. The bad times help us grow and appreciate the good times. I'm learning new things all the time, in all different areas of my life. Throughout all the pressures we put on ourselves and we allow other people to put on us, I've learned to be gentle with myself. We are so hard on ourselves about everything little thing. For example, we judge ourselves for being single at the age of 30 or not having kids by 30, or not having a certain amount of money in the bank by the age of 30. As if 30 is the magical age we are supposed to have life figured out at, when actually, 30 is just the beginning. We are so worried about how others judge us and what they think about us. We stress ourselves out and cause our blood pressure to rise and other health conditions because we are always comparing ourselves to others or not happy with our own outcomes. This book is about forgiving yourself, stepping into your confidence, and not being so hard on yourself. Yes, put a little pressure sometimes, but also, know your capabilities and your situation and create a better future for yourself and your family!

A little bit about me

In case you are wondering whose book you are reading, who is this petite, young black lady telling me to be gentle with myself. Well let me tell you!

You are talking to a woman that overcame fear and stepped out on faith to follow her dreams. She doesn't let nobody stop her. Not her child, a job or judgment from others. She combs through obstacles no matter the circumstances.

You are talking to a woman that didn't mind risking her body to get a better life for her and her son. No, not that! It's not what you think! You must keep reading to find out!

You are talking to woman who knows how to get what she wants, no matter what she must do!

We will be learning how to not let our own fear and lack of confidence, obstacles and outside influences stop us or deter us from being our best selves! My motto for life is Be Gentle with Yourself, and I'm going to show you how. I'm just getting started and there is still so much more to come. So, let's get into it!

Ask and you shall receive, seek and you shall find, knock and the door shall be open to you.

Matthew 7:7

For everyone who asks receives; he who seeks finds; and to him that knocks, the door will be opened

Matthew 7:8

Chapter 1

Confidence

Confidence is the foundation for your success. It's the foundation for who you are, how you act, how you present yourself and so forth. We must believe we deserve the things we desire sis. It's also the foundation of this book. I want to discuss how we need the confidence to do anything before we discuss anything else. From my experience, the first thing we need to make it in this world is confidence. The power of believing. Even God wants you to have faith in him and we can't even see him. We need to have faith in ourselves too. Trust ourselves and our judgment on things we experience and the decisions we have to make, especially challenging ones. Confidence that we make great decisions. Confidence that we are great mothers. Confidence that we are good at our job, confidence to get that degree, confidence to start that business, confidence to be unapologetically you.

Step 1 to anything in life:

1. Believe, believe in yourself, believe it can happen, believe you are worthy of it.

The number one reason a lot of people don't follow their dreams is fear. Fear of failure, fear of embarrassment, fear of losing everything trying to start something. I'm with you sis, I have several fears myself. Have you ever tried imaging your life without fear? Without those fears you have that are stopping you from doing something you are thinking about often. Imagine what life would be like if you didn't have this fear. How can we get rid of this fear. Let's pinpoint what exactly the fear is. Take a moment and think about the life you want. Then ask yourself what's stopping you. Why are we letting that *thing* hold us back? No, really, please take a moment.

Some people call it an excuse, but I'm here to tell you to be gentle with yourself. They're not excuses, its fear. We are scared. Even when it comes to love, we are scared. Scared of getting hurt, scared of being used, fear of the broken heart, scared of looking stupid in front of our friends and family. We are scared to change majors in college, or job careers, or trying new things. Some people are scared of heights, not me, but I can imagine the fear is falling off of something and hurting yourself really bad, maybe even leading to death.

First, we need to start by telling ourselves we deserve it. Whatever that *it* is, if you want it, you deserve it. You deserve to live that dream. You deserve love, you deserve wealth, you deserve to be happy. Loving yourself and telling yourself you are worthy of the things you desire.

I'm no expert, but I'm sure confidence is something we all struggle with, or have struggled with. I don't believe anyone is fully confident. Like 100 percent confident in every aspect of life. If you are, write a book and help a sister out! Sometimes we can be confident in one area and not the other. For example, I know I am pretty, but am I smart? I am a mom, but am I a good mom? I am a saleswoman but am I a good saleswoman? I'm enrolled at this fancy school, but should I be here? Is this school for people like me?

We question ourselves daily about almost everything. I was once an extremely confident, strong woman and then all of a sudden, over a short span of time, events occurred in my life that stripped my confidence away. I'm sure you can relate. Sometimes life happens and we began to question ourselves. I had to build my confidence back up experience after experience. Things that tore my confidence down were things I would read on social media, relationships, friendships, motherhood and my lack of education. Throughout this book we are going to talk about all those things and what I did to rebuild myself to be secure, happy and confident all over again.

Get Cocky with it

You notice how rappers are cocky? Drake, Future, Young Dolph just to name a few. In their raps, they call themselves the best everything. We all know D.J. Khaled says he's the best. Even the rapper that we never heard of, we listen to one of his songs and he's bragging about himself in the song and how great he is. Females rap about how they have the best you know what and how it's so good, he bought you a house and a Bentley. Kanye West is probably the cockiest of them all, in my opinion. In an interview a lady asked him, "*If someone told you a year ago that today you'd be sitting here nominated for 10 Grammy Awards, would you have believed it?*" his response was " *No, what happened is, I actually told other people and they didn't believe it*". That was the response nobody expected. Honestly, I love a cocky man. Yes, I said it. A healthy cocky, if that's a thing. As a alpha woman, I'm naturally attracted to secure and ambitious men that believe in themselves. Men that know how to make anything happen. People that don't believe they deserve their dream life would call this a fairy tale.

They teach us growing up that you shouldn't be cocky or conceited, it's even in the bible not to worship thyself and don't be self-centered and blah blah blah. If you grew up in church like me, like, never skipped a Sunday, you probably don't have a cocky bone in your body. They made sure to tell us to not worship ourselves. But honestly, in this tough world, you must be cocky baby girl. You must be 10 toes down for you! Let's use the word overconfident. No one likes the cocky conceited person right. I'm not telling you to become cocky or conceited, I want you to become overconfident. It's all about verbiage. Even if you are cocky or conceited just don't be obnoxious about it. Inspire others to build their confidence with the confidence you have. Everywhere I go, people tell me I'm pretty, some people even stare at me for long periods of time and it becomes very awkward. I'm so serious, ask my close friends. However, I never let that get to my head. I live in a popular metroplex, there are beautiful women everywhere. My beauty is one of my strengths, but I remain humble in that. Display that and inspire others to be humble in their strengths.

Anytime you're feeling down and insecure, listen to trap music. This sounds silly, but trap music is one of the things that helped me believe in myself. All they talk about is themselves and how they work so hard to get to where they are and how people need to show them some respect. Next thing you know you went from sad and crying in the shower and now you're rapping along passionately because you felt the pain and celebration in almost every lyric in the song. *"I had to grind like that to shine like this"*. *"When I bought that Aston Martin, y'all thought it was rented"-Meek Mill.* Yea you know the song. Feeling accomplished but misunderstood, go listen to that song. Dreams and

Nightmares by Meek Mill. The feeling music gives you may only last for a moment, but it's so helpful. Girl, anytime you're feeling down about yourself- listen to female rap music. Spotify has a playlist called "Feeling Myself". It's all female rappers and it's a huge self-esteem/confidence booster. Lizzo is a good artist to listen to as well if you need a self-esteem booster. Not only does she sing about being a big girl, she also sings about being single and loving herself. So yes, sis, I can relate!

Here are a few songs I listen to when I'm feeling down or like I failed or simply need a self-esteem booster

> *I Love Me- Meghan Trainor*
> *God is a Woman- Ariana Grande*
> *Survivor- Destiny's Child*
> *Beautiful- Bazzi, Camila Cabelo*
> *Girl on Fire-Alicia Keys*
> *Scuse Me- Lizzo*
> *I Am- Baby Tate and Flo Milli*
> *Lizzos' whole album named: Cuz I Love You*

Keep the Comparisons

Imagine how boring life would be if we were all the same. Like really, imagine. There would be no culture, we would all speak the same language, it would be just completely boring. No reason to travel, besides scenery. Nobody to laugh with since we would all have the same personality. No one to love because they are different, no polar opposites, no ying to your yang because you would both be a yang or ying. Do you see what I'm saying sis? We are all different and should appreciate our differences. I absolutely love being different from you. I love that you are different from me. I love being a brown skinned girl. I love my laugh, my voice, my professionalism, I love that I like to read, my ability to be optimistic and 100 other things I love about myself and you should too sis. Love who you are. I used to compare myself to others all the time, so I know the feeling. It's quite natural actually, but once you notice yourself doing it, pause in that moment and think about what you appreciate in that person and what you appreciate about yourself and value the differences.

When you find yourself comparing yourself to others, try to turn it around. When I find myself comparing my son to other children, I actually use that as motivation. When I see another sever year old microwaving his own food, then I know it's time to teach my son to microwave his own food. The old me would be upset that my son doesn't know how to microwave his own food, or get upset at myself because now I have thoughts in my head that's maybe he is spoiled. When really, I'm just being a mom and making my son some food. However, it is good to teach him how to do things for himself and introducing independence. Don't compare yourself, instead, find inspiration in what you see that you like.

All my singles- don't compare yourself to couples. You are single, you are one, and that's okay. No need to compare yourself to a family of two or four. You hear me sis?! I used to do this a lot before I realized what I was doing. I would look at families and think to myself, *wow they have a house, a nice car, 3 pets and babies, how can they afford all that? Better yet, have the time and energy to have 3 pets and children.* Then I realized, oh, because they help each other. If you are one, how can you compare yourself to two? Instead, be inspired. Turn that energy into aspirations. You may be doing this alone, but you got this! God will send a partner soon, someone reliable and trustworthy. Notice I said partner, because this person that you do life with doesn't have to be a lover. You don't have to have an intimate relationship with your soul mate. This could be a very best friend. In the meantime, be inspired, don't be mad. Create a list of things you want to accomplish when you find your partner. I'll share mine; when I find my ideal partner, I would love for us to buy a timeshare together or a beach house. Aspirations, not comparisons.

Another thing sis, try to refrain from comparing your financial status to others. Especially people with different responsibilities then you. Especially without knowing the details, which we shouldn't know anyways, since it's none of our business. As mothers, we have expenses that people without children don't have. Students have expenses that non-students don't have. Is that a word? Non students?! Oh, well, I'm leaving it here! People with sick or older parents may have expenses that others don't have. You understand what I'm saying sis? I know sometimes it's frustrating looking at "Brittany" with no kids, going to Rome or getting Botox every 2 weeks, when maybe we can't because we have a few extra bills that we have to take care of. Just stay in your lane and focus on yourself. We staying in our lane sis. Little do we know, Ms. Brittany went to Rome on a credit card she can't afford to pay back, or maybe she won a free trip at work for being such a great performer. Maybe the trip was a gift, or maybe she been putting in overtime or working hard on that side hustle to go to Rome. Point is, focus on you. We don't compare ourselves to others, we congratulate people for the things they have going on and possibly let it inspire us. If you see someone doing some of the things you would like to do in life, ask them how they do it. Maybe they came up with a specific side hustle to pay for that *thing* they love. Know your situation and your capabilities and don't compare yourself to others in a negative light. Don't hate, celebrate. Collaborate.

Although social media is a great way to keep up with our friends and family, limiting the time you spend on social media can help limit the comparisons. I'll say it again in this book, but it's hard trying to lose weight or keep your figure when everyone on social media is drinking margaritas all day. Or eating donuts and ice cream at the cutest, newest shop in the city. It's hard to study and discipline yourself when every time you log on, everyone else is partying and going on vacation again. We all love social media, some of us are addicted to it and don't even realize it. I couldn't even stay logged out for seven days, so I'm with you sis. It's the perfect time waster while waiting in line at Walmart for your turn at self-checkout. It's also a great way to learn new things if you are using it to learn and be inspired, but do that and log off. Try to limit your scrolling, by setting some screen time limits on your phone. Www.BCC.com recommends not checking your phone, i.e., social media, first thing in the morning and not being on it at least one hour before bed. WEBMD.COM did a study on 154 participants and studies show that even taking a one week break from social media promoted better sleep and had significant improvements from anxiety and depression. If you don't do it for yourself at least do it for your kids sis. Limit the time your child spends on the internet. The same way you may be subconsciously comparing yourself to others on the internet, our kids are doing the same and it could affect their mental health. A word!

We can go on and on, on many reasons why we shouldn't compare ourselves, but you get the point. You don't need to compare yourself to her, him, them or whoever else. Even your kids. Don't compare yourself to no one, your kids or your family. We all learn at our own pace. We all have different things going on, different responsibilities, we are all on different journeys. Accept and admire your current season. Only compare yourself to yourself. The 2013 you to the 2022 you. I look at how far I've grown over the years and love who I've become and so should you sis. Of course, there is always room for growth, in every category of life.

Self-Worth

Let's start with how we view ourselves. On the inside. Yes girl, our self-esteem. How do you feel about yourself? How do others make you feel? We need to be confident in how we feel about ourselves first. Not just about looks, but how we allow others to treat us as well. Here's the part you've been waiting for. The things that tore my confidence down. Don't worry, I didn't get too deep on you. We'll save that for the next book!

For a long time, I was made fun of for being skinny. Bigger people would make side slick comments like "that skinny b*tch". Sometimes you can call out the jealousy, but even then, it still stings a little, especially when it's people I care about. A major reason it stings is because I can't say anything back. Well, I can, but I like to keep the peace. I'm too grown and too cute to be out here fighting, because we all know, once I call you fat, there's a high chance there will be a fight. Somehow, the world determined it's not rude to call someone skinny or small, but it's rude to call someone big or fat. People call me skinny as if I said "God, make me skinny" and he granted my wish. I was born skinny. I had to buy my breast for goodness sake! Skinny people get made fun of too. All my childhood people called me "Skinny Minnie". They called me anorexic and would ask what do I eat and where does it go, Oh and don't ever throw up! Someone sees you throwing up and would say "that's why you skinny". They had the jokes, "you so little I thought you was a pole standing there". A lot of skinny people are sometimes insecure about being skinny due to eating disorders or anorexia, and here you are commenting on my weight. I can't gain weight to save my life. I tried it, didn't work. The most weight I've ever gained is five to ten pounds and the very next week it'll come right off without me even trying. But the moment I call you "fat" it's going to be a problem, right? Now imagine if I was walking around commenting on people weight the same way they comment on mine. Like "Hey you fatty, how's your day"?! Now I'm the one being rude right? First of all, that is not a way to greet people. Why is that the first thing that comes out of our mouth? Is how big or small someone is? No one wants to be constantly told how they are "supposed" to look, whether you're skinny or not. I had to learn how to let the skinny jokes fly off my shoulder. As I'm sure the bigger girls had to learn how to let the fat jokes fly off theirs. Now small jokes here and there are fine, I understand a joke and can laugh as well. Once I learned how to accept these comments, I really started to accept myself. Like, yea I am skinny, and I love my skinny self. I say this to say, we have to be happy with who we are, no matter what people say about us. Being happy and accepting of yourself on the inside leads to the outside. Don't allow other people's insecurities to project onto your self-esteem. I've learned some people talk mess because they may envy the thing they are talking about. Don't let other people's opinion of you determine your self-worth. How about we all just complement each other, big or small and give each other a hug and say you look good today! That dress fits you very well and you look good sis!

Speaking of looks, sometimes I find myself dressing down depending on who I'm going to hang out with, because I didn't want to be "too pretty", and make others feel uncomfortable. I would get dressed up and be myself and people would say "it's not a fashion show

Nisha" or "I said casual". This led to me wanting to dress down more. However, when I dress down, I don't feel like I'm being myself. I don't feel like I'm presenting myself in my best manner. Which is now leading_to a confidence problem or simply being uncomfortable because I'm not being myself? So that was me being nice, being humble. Trying to make sure I don't make others uncomfortable around me just because of the way I look. The truth is, we should never dim our light for others, we should never dress down because others are uncomfortable, we should never be less than to make others comfortable. Chanel Ayan from Housewives of Dubai sure didn't bring herself down to please others. They even claimed she looked better than the bride at one point. Bring that leadership role out and lead the way. Make them come up to your level. Yes, our level sis! They should be dressing up to come see us. Period. As I am writing this book, I literally decided that I'm no longer bringing myself down to make others feel comfortable. When we get dressed, we are representing ourselves. Especially as black women. As a black woman, I represent black women when I leave the house or show up on social media. If I'm out the country, I represent my country. Think about that. Why are we not dressing up and looking our best sis? Especially on vacation. At least look somewhat fly. *Dress the way you want to be addressed- Bianca Frazier,* I'm not saying we can't wear sweats to go grab some milk at the store really quick. I am saying; make sure they are cute sweats. Haha. Naw for real though. Some Fashion Nova sweats or something that appreciates your figure. I'm saying, lets study fashion just a little bit and learn how to dress for our body type this way we know what type of clothes to buy so that we can be confident in dressing up to go places. I'm saying, don't bring someone down because you didn't feel like dressing the part that day. These little instances made me realize I no longer want to downplay myself about who I am and how I dress and you shouldn't either sis. Be a leader, be inspiring. That comes to fashion, motherhood, dating and all topics of life. Some people will be insecure around us, but this is a chance to lift someone up and remind them of their own special powers, instead of putting each other down. In the meantime, for our sake, don't let others determine your self-worth. Keep shining sis!

Another thing that brought my confidence down, and I had to work to bring it back up was being with a man. They try to teach us that the man is the man and blah blah blah. It feels like the older we get the more sensitive most men's feelings get. Like we have totally switched roles overtime. Maybe it just these new age guys. I had to learn how to tip toe around the male ego. I'm still learning this in fact. Many women have this complaint actually, but I guess we all want a man in our life, so we have to learn how to be with a man without letting it take down our confidence and who we are on the inside. For example, "men like smart women". Ha! No, they don't! It's just a nice thing to say. Everyone loves a smart person, just don't be smarter than them, right? Now, with that being said, it doesn't mean you have to always correct somebody and I understand that. Never let your ego get in the way of a connection. Most women know this. Just say "Okay" and keep it moving. To avoid arguments, I would literally teach myself how to play dumb and play sly fox and not say anything, boosting his ego and basically silencing myself to make him feel smarter or better. I couldn't be too smart, too loud, can't have opinions, just agree with what he says. Now I know some women reading this have no clue what I'm talking about because maybe you're dating an extremely secure man who lets your light shine and that's great, or on the flip side, you're wearing the pants in your relationship. Or simply, you love your man so much that this isn't a problem for you, and that's great. I loved this man, so I didn't mind boosting him up. Compromise, right? However, in the process it did tear me down on the inside. It actually got a point where I lost myself. Losing yourself is a fear we have when we get into relationships. My "good girl act" became my personality. I went on a date with a new guy that was looking for my black girl magic. My spiciness, my attitude, my opinions, my personality. But now where was my personality? It was gone because my previous boyfriend, trained me to be silent and agreeable. Girl, this is a whole 'nother book! My point is, don't let these men or whoever you're dating, take your confidence and self-esteem levels down. Don't be so submissive that you lose who you are. Healthy submission does exist, just with the right person. I know too many women going through this, so I must speak on it. It's 2022. You are smart, your voice and opinions matter. Your feelings matter. We have to start asking ourselves, are those around us secure in themselves? Recognize when someone is insecure in themselves and they try to gaslight and manipulate you. Insecure ppl are the ones that want to control and manipulate situations. Don't let your spouse silence you, even if you don't see it as an issue. Don't let your spouse determine your self-worth. That's for you to determine. Always. Let's say it together, I AM NO LONGER BELITTLING MYSELF TO MAKE OTHERS COMFORTABLE! THAT INCLUDES MEN AND WOMEN!

If people hate you, then you're probably doing something right

- Amy Lee

When I tell you relationships tore my confidence down, this is what I meant sis. I stopped tooting my own horn aka loving myself <u>out loud</u>. This behavior came from dating insecure masculine men. When in group settings, I never said anything because I didn't want to overshadow my man, or someone's great story, or be the loudest one in the room, or always bragging about myself. Some would say this is a sign that I am secure in who I am, yes, however, I didn't toot my own horn for so long that I forgot how. I forgot how to love myself sis. I would always downplay myself in conversation because I didn't want to seem like that obnoxious "independent woman" who's always bragging about her accomplishments. For example, *"it's just a benz, one of the lower class's "*, or *"Oh, it's just a small house, just enough for me and my son"*. If you always have to downplay who you are or your accomplishments, you're hanging around the wrong people. Let's stop doing this and tell our story! Yes, I got my money together and bought a house so my son can run around in a big backyard! In a room full of educated people and high earners, the things I've accomplished are basic to them. I love hanging out with them. Let me tell you something sis. I live in a two-story home and from the top of the stairs in the playroom I can see almost the whole house from there. Sometimes I go up there and just look at my house. My empire. This beautiful place I created into a home. My decorations, my furniture, Marvel characters and nerf bullets all over the floor and missing remotes. Like I did all this. I did all this by myself. Women marched in the streets for my freedom and I'm pretty sure I can say, I made them proud. I also love being able to have my own money, saving and spending as much as I want without asking! You can always toot your horn when you around me! Toot Toot! Stop sleeping on yourself girl! When we tell our story, you never know who's watching and who's admiring. Be proud of yourself! Admire yourself. Love yourself again and again and never stop. Again, not letting our self-worth come from other people's opinions and insecurities. Not belittling ourselves to make others comfortable. Keep telling your story. Toot your horn sis!

Another thing that stripped my confidence was social media. Yep, let's talk about it. I'm a self-sufficient woman, aka an independent woman. Anything I need, I can provide, anything I require, I can provide, I fully take care of my son with very little financial help. I have and pay for basic necessities on my own. Here's where it turned around. I read on social media one day, this huge long post about how being "ultra-independent" is toxic. The post mentioned you should have someone you can depend on, then led along to say "if you're an independent woman you are a man". Basically, discing independent women. I was in a weak state of mind when I saw that post and it bothered me a lot. I wished I could be less resourceful and depend on men for my well-being, but I wasn't raised like that. Reading that post made me feel like- Why am I being made fun of for making sure I'm not homeless. That's just so weird to me. Now being ultra-independent may be toxic. I don't know if that's a fact. I had to learn to take things I read on social media with a grain of salt. Just read and scroll, laugh and scroll. If the post not for you, keep scrolling sis. This post, however, did have me thinking. Who can I call if I have a flat tire, if I get in an accident or if there's an emergency. I will say, learning how to properly manage my money has made me more independent. I don't need to call a man or my mom and ask for money because my tire popped. I don't need to wait till payday to do anything. If something happens today, I got it, I take care of it, I get it fixed and done. I always managed my money well, even in times it wasn't much of it. Of course, I have my mom and step dad. They are there for me without a doubt. Shout out to them! Growing up, I watched my mom do everything independently, I adopted those same behaviors. I think not having siblings also makes it challenging for me to connect with others which may be why I don't have a big friend group. If I want to go grab dinner and drinks, that's when I call my friends. For parties and fun things. I never wanted to be a burden on people and calling always asking for something. My friend one day was telling me she had to help her sister one day because her car stopped on the road because she ran out of gas. I thought to myself, how cute. I personally can't let that happen because I don't have anyone to call if I run out of gas. That's a Triple A call for me. That's a $100 call for me. Or standing on the street hoping I look cute that day in hopes that a man would walk by and help. Accidents happen for sure, however, I have to be prepared for all my accidents or I'm SOL, out of luck. Maybe being independent is toxic? It's a blessing and a curse, that's for sure. I know somebody reading this feels me right now!

I was in a car accident one day and I cried, not because I was in an accident, but because I had no one to call. The car was slightly damaged, I was ok, shook it off and went about my business. But I was sad. I wanted to be able to call someone and say "I just got in an accident" and hope they come running just to be by my side. So maybe being independent is toxic. Who knows. I took that post offensive at the time because I was insecure about being independent. I look around and everyone has help but me. I would ask God, why do I have to do things alone and everyone else gets help. Why does such a "beautiful woman", as people would say, have to do life alone? I guess we'll never know. However, I can't let social media make me feel bad about being blessed enough to take care of myself and my son. You shouldn't either sis. You're doing a great job. If we think about it on the bright side, we have respect for ourselves. We don't just let anyone in our space. We are not desperate for attention. I know plenty of women who wish they were independent, so we have to be grateful if we are. It's actually an accomplishment. After all, we are adults. Adults should be able to do for themselves. It's all about perspective. Again, could be a blessing, could be a curse.

Speaking of social media, do not let social media determine your worth! Do not determine your self-worth off likes, hearts and how many views or DM's you have. I have a YouTube Channel. I get very little views on my videos, but guess what, sis, I love my videos. I do that for me. I'm funny, I make myself laugh, and I love creating the content for the videos. Filming and editing and posting is all an outlet to make me feel productive. Of course, I'm not going to sit here and pretend that I don't care how many views I get. Yes, I want people to see my work, but I don't let that get me down. I'm still posting, still filming when I want, and that's because that makes me happy. Anytime you're feeling down about yourself, look in the mirror, look at how beautiful you are and tell yourself that you can do anything you put your mind to. That you are capable. Look at what you've accomplished so far. I want you to walk around your place and point out the things you didn't have 3-5 years ago. Even the place itself. That list gone start piling up. Even mentally. Think about the things you used to tolerate versus what you tolerate now. Look at how far you've come! You are worthy! You are enough! We don't need social media to tell us this. This is why it's so important to take breaks from social media or limit the time you spend on social media. Watch who you follow. It's the same thing in real life friendships. You should only be following people and things that inspire you. If you not logging off feeling inspired, you using it wrong.

Don't get your self-worth from other people either. I have learned in this life you cannot please people. "You don't call enough, you don't text back fast enough, you gave me $100 instead of $150". "You didn't tip enough, you didn't pump the gas right, you didn't cook that meal the way my mom does". One thing I have learned in this life is you're doomed if you do, you're doomed if you don't. If I cook this meal for you, the complaint is I didn't make it like your mom does. If I don't cook this meal for you, now I'm lazy and I'm not a good friend or girlfriend. Like what!? People are insatiable. Let them stay in their feelings. You don't get your self-worth based off of people's complaints and feelings towards you. One thing I learned from reading the 4 Agreements, as long as you know you tried your best and you're always trying your best, keep pushing baby.

Don't let your cheating spouse determine your worth either. If your spouse cheats on you, those are demons they have to deal with. You hear me sis? There could be many reasons that person cheated but I strongly believe the biggest reason is a personal insecurity. Or a lack thereof. It has nothing to do with you. If someone cheats, they are the one that fell weak to temptation, they are the one that broke the vow, before you and God, they are the one that deceived you and lied to you. That is their problem. Not yours, be gentle with yourself baby.

"*Protect your energy*"

So, I just opened up to you and told you all the things that tore down my confidence. Friendships, relationships, and more. Oohh, be gentle with me friend. Building my confidence back up wasn't an easy road. It's a process, but with self-help books and God by side, I was able to overcome. Constantly saying my affirmations, daily, in the mirror. Yes, in the mirror. Look at yourself in the mirror and tell yourself your dreams, what you are capable of, that you are enough and you are worthy of the things you desire. I am also learning how to take up for myself. Learning the difference between not needing to have the last word versus taking up for myself. Talking to my friends/people, telling them how I feel and if something bothered me. This is actually a journey. I'm hoping I can help someone today. Here are some other ways to build confidence. I wanted confidence to be the first chapter of this book because it's the foundation of you. You must have confidence to do everything else we will be discussing in this book. and you have to believe in yourself. I hope to be able to guide the path to believing in yourself.

How to get confident

Part of being confident is getting things done. Decide who and what you want to be, what you want out of life- create a vision and get it done. Make a checklist. Write things down that you would like to accomplish. Even if you feel like it's something little, girl, just add it on the list. Make weekly checklist, monthly checklist, yearly or life checklist. Even if it seems out of this world, write and down and aim towards it. When you do it, place a checkmark by the item. Just looking at checkmarks on your paper makes you feel accomplished or like you're on your way to bigger things. Even consider the small goals to get to the big goals. Don't forget the small goals.

Creating a vision and a mission statement can help us stay focused on what we want. It's easy to say no to things that don't align with our goals. I get invited to a lot of events because people see me as a happy, go getter, that likes to meet people and make money. One day I was invited to go to an event where they said you can learn how to make money. I went, I was excited to network and learn something new. I was selling my detox tea at this time, so meeting new people was crucial for my success. I arrived and discovered it was about selling life insurance. I was a little disappointed but happy to even be in the room with like-minded people. We all want financial freedom, however, selling life insurance wasn't it for me. I actually had a friend at the time who sold life insurance, was really good at it, making $3000+ checks at 21 years old. I was happy for her but it was not for me. Because of this, it was easy for me to turn down the opportunity. I was already passionate about selling my detox tea, I didn't see myself sitting at peoples' living room tables at 7pm on a Wednesday, explaining whole life and term life policies. That wasn't my passion. Which leads me back to my point. If you know you want to own a mechanic shop and or fix cars for a living and someone comes to you with a corporate job opportunity or help them sell some skin care products, you can easily say no to them because you know what your end goal is. Selling skin care products may not align with your goal to fix cars or own your own mechanic shop one day. Having a clear vision, helps you stay focused.

A mission statement can look like: *I strive to be an amazing mom and will be a great role model to my son and others. I will inspire people all across the world to believe in themselves and strive for a better life. I will travel the world and create the most dope memories with my son, family and friends. I will always strive to remain fit and active and be mindful of what I put in my body. I will maintain a relationship with*

God no matter what. I will not burn bridges with valuable people. I will always push myself to make minimum five figures a month. I will be an investor and create wealth and teach my son to be a leader. I will strive to help others however I can. I will give back to my community either through volunteer or donations. I will be an amazing wife one day to an amazing man, we will be healthy in love. I will strive to operate all my relationships (friends and intimate ones) off love and not off ego. I will be wise and humble.

Notice on some items I said "I will strive"...that's what makes it a mission. A mission statement is writing your vision out for your life. I will try to do this, I will strive to do that. I will push myself. "I will be" those are things I know I can do. Sometimes we will have crazy days or gaps in our life where we are lazy with our goals and that's okay. Write it down, type it out, print it out, hang it up, frame it, you can even place it on your vision board! Hang it up in the mirror with some of your affirmations and love notes. Your mission statement should be somewhere close to your vison board so you can constantly see it. When you feel yourself falling off, read your mission statement out loud to yourself and remember what type of person you want to be and the things you want to accomplish. Reading this constantly or seeing it hanging up somewhere should keep you on track.

Back to my vision. It actually took me a year to find a house. I knew I wanted a garden tub, big backyard space, 3-4 bedrooms and 2 car garage. All of this I wrote down in my five-year goals by the way. I was very specific. My agent showed me homes with small backyards and no garden tub and it was easy for me to say no to those homes because those homes didn't align with my vision. I stayed firm with what I wanted and didn't settle until I found my perfect home. When I look back, It seems like I manifested that home, I knew exactly what

I wanted and got it. Saying no to things that don't serve you, helps you stay focused on your end goal. When you are focused, it allows you to be more confident.

Being fearless also goes along with having confidence, you have to be willing to take chances. I actually found a different house before I bought the house that I actually live in. It was a cute condo, in the city I grew up in, by my son's school, everything was perfect-but the mortgage payment was going to be double than what I was paying in rent and that scared the crap out of me, even though I could afford it according to my approval letter. The home I actually live in now, the payment scared me as well, but I told myself, you know what, this is what you want, this is what you saved money for, this is the house, it has everything, so I placed my offer with a motivation letter and got the house. Buying a home is one of the biggest purchases you'll make in life so of course there was that natural fear, but imagine if I let fear just keep putting me down. I would still be in that small 800 square foot apartment with one full bathroom with a leak in the ceiling every time it rained. I had to take a chance. I took the chance, never missed a payment, and never looked back. Step out on faith, sis. Don't let your fears hold you back, ever.

Confidence is also not caring so much what others think. You should think of yourself as the person people want to be. Like a leader, the teacher, a person that inspires others. Of course, it's natural to value opinions of loved ones, but for the most part, focus on what makes you happy babe. If people don't support you, just keep it to yourself, no need to take it personal. What they don't know, they can't ruin. How I remove negativity from my head is asking myself the famous question. "Do they pay my bills". Some people would say, well what does bills have to do with anything. What we are really saying when we ask people this question is, "Do they assist me with my lively hood? Do they even have their life together, are they even happy? Do they help me take my son to school and his activities? Do they help me sleep at night, are they there for me when I'm sick?" "Is dinner on the table when I get home? Do you sign my check"! That's what we really saying. Those are the real questions we need to ask ourselves before we get so caught up in others' opinions of us. I always consider the source as well. If someone is trying to judge your life or decisions, take a look at their life to see if its better, and ifs it not, then you can determine if you want to take that advice or judgement or opinions. Like real talk, always consider the source.

"Envision the woman you want to be. Act like her, speak like her, dress like her, exercise like her, study like her, embody her, think like her. Eventually you will become her. You will be proud of her"

-Sheneka Adams

Of course, we all have our bad days and we don't feel like we are enough, or incapable of something, but one thing I always tell myself is "be gentle with yourself". You are enough, just exactly the way you are and sometimes when you are feeling down, think about how far you've come, think about how hard you tried, or trying, no matter what it is. Whether its motherhood, a job, trying to work it out with a spouse, school, whatever scenario, if you tried hard then you should be proud. I think of Khloe Kardashian. The whole world watched her get cheated on multiple times by the same man, but she put on a brave face and worked on that relationship. I'm sure for her family, for the sake of love and forgiveness and giving him a chance to grow, learn and mature. We all want the family unit. Most woman want it *real bad*. She tried her hardest. I say this to say, as long as you know you tried your hardest and you aren't the problem or things just didn't work out the way you wanted, be proud of yourself. Find a reason to smile at the good times. You are the author of your story; you have the power to create the change you want to see in your life. Let people talk, let haters hate, don't apologize for being you! Be Gentle with yourself.

"If you can look in the mirror and say I did everything I could, did I do everything possible to try and get better? If the answer is yes, let the dust settle where it may"

- Kobe Bryant

Affirmations for confidence:

- *I am enough*
- *I am capable of ___*
- *I believe in myself*
- *I am protected*
- *I forgive myself*
- *I am a great mom and role model*
- *I am powerful and fearless*
- *I am smart and resourceful*
- *Its ok to be feminine and ambitious*
- *Being independent does not make me masculine*
- *I let go of fear, worry and blame*
- *I let go of everything that does not serve me on my journey*
- *I love my life, myself and those around me*
- *I am committed to myself and my goals*
- *I am wise and humble*
- *I am valuable*
- *I am proud of who I am*
- *I am worthy of everything I desire*
- *I believe in my ability to manifest*
- *I am not dimming my light to make others feel comfortable*

Chapter 2

Ambition

From food stamps to fresh fruit on yachts baby! Yes, we made it! Let me tell you how it started!

Well, first of all, I was fired from my first job. Yep, working at CiCi's Pizza, I was 16 years old, they fired me because I wasn't moving fast enough for them. Isn't that something? Of course, they gave me warning and coaching and I tried and tried but I guess I still wasn't passing out orders quick enough for them. Let me tell you something honey, I never got fired again for being slow! Now, I don't know if this is good or bad, but now I move with a since of urgency, ever since that day and I truly believe it led to my success.

Fast forward, now I'm 20 years old and not only was I living with my mom, but now I'm pregnant. Not only did I need to move out, but I started researching childcare cost and baby formula and realized I needed to get a good paying job. That job couldn't come quick enough. I had my baby, and I was stuck at the WIC office for hours waiting on them to give me money to feed my baby. Any man that has dated me will tell you, I'm not good at waiting on others. If I need something, I need it now. Especially if it's for my baby, you feel me? Also, I don't know about you, but spending half a day at a WIC office was not fun for me. Although I was so grateful for the help and assistance that WIC has to provide, because it's an excellent program by the way, but I needed to keep steady with the job hunt. Stay focused on the goal. Besides, the program isn't permanent help, so I needed a backup plan.

I remember my sons first doctors' appointment at this nasty doctor's office. It was his one-week checkup. His father had to work so my mother was kind enough to join me. We walked in and it smelled bad. Like really bad, children coughing and crying everywhere in the waiting room. It was loud, I couldn't hear myself talk and the wait time was over an hour. Then when it was finally our turn, the doctor didn't wash her hands or put hand sanitizer before she touched my baby. Girl, I almost lost it. As soon as we left that doctors office, my mom and I both exchanged a look and said "never again". If this is the doctors that Medicaid is providing, I quickly saw that I needed to get more steady on the job hunt to get a good job so that I can get good health insurance so that I never have to step in that doctors office again.

My mom joined the hunt, telling all her friends to look out for job openings. Someone said Capital One Bank was hiring, I applied and there I started my first corporate job! Thanks Mom! I don't really think my mom realizes how much I appreciate her until she reads this book and I spell it all out! I was on government assistant for about 6 months until my paychecks started rolling in good at my new job. I graduated from Medicaid sis! We never saw that doctor's office again. We love Noah's new doctor and still go to her till this day. I do still miss WIC from time to time. Free cheese!? Man, what!! Medicaid and food stamps, are all great programs, but they are there to give you a boost in life. It was just the booster I needed. Thanks America.

Ambition: The inner drive to succeed and thrive at ones goal and purpose.

Having or showing a strong desire and determination to succeed.

Two to three years later, I'm well into working my jobs and growing my career but it still wasn't enough. I had just become a single mother at this time and needed more money. With no college degree or no real skills, I searched and searched online about what I can do. I was living in a two-bedroom apartment, with my step sister as my roommate and even though she was helping with the rent, it just never seemed to be enough. Search after search online, I came across an ad that said get paid to become a surrogate mother. I thought about it for a few months, read a lot of reviews and did some research. Even flew to California (on their dime, sis) to meet up with them and see if I liked what they are doing. *Do I really want to risk my whole life to have a baby for someone else,* I thought to myself. Women can lose their lives giving birth. Then a year went by and the rent went up. The daycare fee went up as well and it was made clear to me that I would be the one responsible for paying it. I had already cut down on so many other bills so at this point, I needed to get a second job. Worked two jobs for a few months, not only did this raise the cost of childcare, but now I have no time to spend with my child. Becoming a surrogate mother started to sound really attractive. Plus, I get to help someone! I've always been a saver, but the little money I did have, it was going to run out soon and I knew eventually I wanted to buy a home. I needed to find a way to get more money to fund all these dreams I had. So, I called the Surrogacy Agency and told them I'm in! Did I just do something crazy? I was hopping on planes to get medicine and go to doctor appointments, I was injecting myself in the buttocks to get pregnant and stay pregnant and yes, I was going through morning sickness and taking extreme good care of my body all for someone else. Yes, sis, I became a surrogate mother. Now that's what I call doing something strange for a piece of change. Well, a big piece of change in this case. I didn't even have my mother's support at first. She said she didn't want to see me throughout the whole pregnancy. She didn't agree with my decision at all. Although I wanted my mother's support, I knew this was something I needed to do for me and my son. I knew that my job was just a job and I would be stuck here forever if I don't make a change now. Even if that means risking my body and my life to make sure my son is taken care of. So, I kept the surrogacy secret to myself and eventually gained my mother's support. I even met my new boyfriend at this time and he was very supportive! Isn't that something?! If you're still single, try getting pregnant, you might find a man! Anyways, I say this to say, with no degree and no other real skills, I did what I thought I needed to do to get out the rat race and get another booster in life. I'm always looking for my next move. You've heard it before, get uncomfortable to get comfortable. I'm not telling you to do it, I'm just telling my story.

Did the surrogacy thing and actually made a new friend. I still keep in contact with the parents. Got paid and everything but what's next? I've always been ambitious. I knew it was time to go in a new direction when one day I heard an ad on the radio saying they will teach me how to invest in real estate for free. Now, I know I'm not the only one who watches HGTV and get so inspired watching people flip houses and making five to six figures checks off one flip. The radio ad said come to this free seminar and we will teach you everything you need to know! What's there to lose right? It's free. Let me just go see what they are talking about. I was a little late to my own son's birthday party coming from this seminar. That's how serious I wanted another change in my life. I went to this free two-hour seminar and they didn't really tell us how to flip houses. If you want to learn how to flip houses, you needed to go to the next seminar which was "$3000 but we will give it to you today for $1500". There was no hesitation for me.

Although I didn't have $1500, my bank did. Girl, I swiped that credit card so fast! (Now, I know what you're thinking sis, but the surrogacy process took about a year until I actually got pregnant and started getting paid.) At this event they gave us some books to read, some audio to listen to, notebook and a laptop bag. I went home and read all the books, listened to all the audio, two or three times might I add, I even wrote a business plan down and presented it to my mom within the coming weeks. My boyfriend at the time said I was stupid for spending that money, we could have used that money for household bills and blah blah blah, but till this day, I don't regret my decision! Some people call it a scam, and of course I can see why, but this "scam" was the beginning of my real estate career.

So, I paid the $1500 for the next seminar which was a 3-day seminar for 8 hours a day. I took time off from work to go to this seminar. At the next seminar they had some really inspiring guest speakers and showed us a little bit about how to flip houses, but if you wanted to learn more, the next seminar was $30,000. I stopped there. I got the information I needed for now and let's work from there. Plus, I didn't have $30,000, but I watched so many people burrow money from their retirement and credit cards to go to the next seminar where they promise to make you a millionaire. Again, some may see this as a scam, I'm not completely oblivious, but I was happy with my decision. While others are spending $80,000 at colleges, I got everything I needed for $1500. Sounded like a good investment to me. Never be afraid to invest in education sis. Any kind. Whether it's going to seminars to learn from the locals, or community college courses, or even courses on Instagram and YouTube always stay learning. Stay ambitious.

At the seminar I met a lady who has her own real estate group in Dallas. I started going to her meetings and events. I literally called off work to go to her luncheons. They would meet Thursdays for lunch and sometimes Tuesdays for dinner. I would bring my son on Tuesday nights because I didn't have a babysitter. Yep, I sure did. He was the only kid there, as always when it comes to my business stuff, and while everyone else was standing up to introduce themselves, I would stand up and introduce the both of us. I would bring paper and crayons so he could color or sometimes give him my phone while I take notes in the meeting. I wasn't letting my child stop me from learning how to get rich! The host of the meetings, her name was Ms. Cathy, she would have guest speakers at her meetings, people passed out their business cards and it was basically a real estate community. There would be Private money lenders, hard money lenders, title companies, property management companies, home owners' insurance company spokespersons at these meetings, like it was the real deal. She offered different classes where she taught different topics about real estate, such as wholesaling, property taxes, how to sign paperwork and more. I met some business owners and networked so much. I went out and made my own business cards to start passing out too so I can fit in with the crowd. I actually tried to flip a house once but fear got the best of me and I backed out. I went to her meetings for about 2 years. All for free, I didn't pay another dime. On Saturday mornings, sometimes they had meetings at different houses and would walk you through the house and tell you how to flip that particular house. I learned so much, took so many notes, rented so many books from the library about real estate and bought some too. I was invited to other seminars in the area from people that traveled to host in different states. Now these local seminars were like $80 to attend and I always saw it as in investment. I will forever pay money to learn with no regrets. I even learned how to run an elderly community. Basically, learning the million ways to make money in real estate. This is what led me to working in the mortgage industry.

Due to always calling off work to go to these meetings, my manager at the time saw my new found love and ambition for real estate and offered me a job at a mortgage company. Yep, he quit a little before me, then once he got to the company, he offered me to come follow him at his new company. So, we both left our job at Bank of America to go work in the mortgage industry. On top of that, this new job was paying $10,000 more a year than what I was currently making. That's a win win! They say it's all about who you know!

I started this new job as a processor. A loan processor. You're starting to see a pattern now. I don't stop, do I? Fast forward to now I'm a loan officer. I now been working in mortgage industry for over 6 years now, 2 years a purchase loan officer. Being a loan officer changed my life! Now let me tell you how *that* started.

After three years of being a loan processor, I would take walks around the building at work on my breaks. I started noticing Corvettes, BMW's, Porsches in the parking lot and was like, well I'm definitely working in the wrong department! Again, thankful for the opportunity, but don't get comfortable on them sis. What's next in life for me? I knew my salary couldn't afford a Porsche and I did not become a surrogate mother to buy a fancy car. What's a girl gotta do?! I started asking questions, like what position do I need to be able to afford a luxury car? I started meeting people in different departments, using my networking skills I learned at those real estate meetings, and they told me exactly what to do. I followed the instructions and here I am today! *"Broke black ni**a, remember me? Until I found out that* *recipe. Started getting bout ten a week, finger on the trigger when I sleep".* -Young Dolph. I love Young Dolph! RIP. Now back to the point, I started making four figure bonus' that lead to five figure bonus'. Bonus'. That means on top of base pay. As I got better at the job, the checks started getting bigger. I couldn't believe it! I would cry on paydays. Like what's happening? I was officially a six-figure earner. That business plan I told you I presented to my mom, I told her I would be a six-figure earner and it's happening. Honestly when I said it, I'm sure she didn't believe me, shoot, I didn't really even believe myself. I knew it would happen eventually, but I didn't think I can do it before I turned 30. Let alone at a job. I would read all these books that talk about entrepreneurship, and how you need to own your own business if you want to make good money. So, I had it stuck in my mind that I needed to flip houses, or own a business in order to make good money and I was discouraged for a long time. So, when I started making this good money at a W2 job, without a degree and the schedule fit in with the school schedule, 9-5, I knew God was on my side. Can we say #winning. The entrepreneurs had me thinking working a job was not the way to freedom. I guess you just have to find a good job. I've met so many people who work jobs that make anywhere from $300k – millions a year at a W2 employer. We all know the man who was fired from ERCOT in Texas in 2021 when the state froze over because we had no power. www.ksat.com reported his salary as $803k a year. Of course, he was an engineer with a degree, I'm sure. I was once a loan processor and I saw, with my own two eyes, a W2 for a lady making $635k/ year as a Human Resource VP at AT&T or Spectrum, I forgot which company it was. I once dated a guy that salary at his job was around $500k. He worked for Frigidaire. My point is, $500- $800k a year sounds good to me. The men in my books made it seem impossible to make unless I owned my own business. I'm not telling you to go get a corporate job, I'm telling you, my story. I'm also saying don't count it out of your options. Curiosity didn't kill this cat. I'm so glad I was curious, ambitious, and tenacious.

What is a loan officer you ask? A loan officer is a licensed loan professional that can get you pre-approved for a mortgage to buy a home. Yep! That's what I do. I write loans. In order to become a loan officer, you have a take a 20-hour course, I took 23 hours since apparently, I'm an overachiever, and pass the state exam, which is extremely hard, and bam! You are a licensed loan officer once you find a company to sponsor you. Which means find a job. When you are ready to buy a house, you call a bank to try to get pre-qualified. Once you send them proof that you can afford the loan, such as bank statements to prove your assets, tax returns, paystubs, W2's and such to prove your income, this pre-qualification will be upgraded to a pre-approval. The person to get that done, is a loan officer. Some companies call it a mortgage professional, loan originator, and a real fancy one is account executive. We can be called many things but most people know it as a loan officer. After you get pre-approved and find a house, the day it closes and you get the keys, once the loan funds, the loan officer get paid. I knew I wanted to get involved in real estate because it seems like everyone in the deal can win. The person buying the house, the seller, the real estate agent, if you have one, the appraiser, the escrow agent, and the loan officer. Everyone in the transaction got something out of the deal.

As a loan officer, you still have to hustle like a business owner. That's why I like it. The more you want to make, the more clients you have to take. If you're really tenacious, you would go out and source your own clients instead of sitting at your desk waiting for the company to help your phone ring.

Loan Officers and corporate executives have the potential to make more than a surgeon would, more than professors and ppl who went to college for years to do that job. To be a loan officer, you literally have to have a high school diploma/GED and pass a test to get certified. I took those steps and added this money to my surrogacy money now we're eating fresh fruit on yachts! I wanted to start this book off just giving you a background of my profession and background of me because it's important to know how I got here. What I do for a living is a reflection of who I am. Not only am I able to make decent money and change the trajectory of my lifestyle, but I'm able to connect with people, help them follow their dreams of owning their first home, or their first investment property, or their forever home, meet new people all the time, look at amazing houses-which I love to do and that's not even a requirement for the job, I just love houses, most importantly, I'm able to help people. Even being a surrogate mother, was me helping someone. I am writing this book because I want to help you, inspire you and I hope to encourage you to be curios and ambitious and go get what's waiting for you! Telling you how I started and hoping that you can start your dreams! Tell people your dreams and ask for help. My initial dream wasn't to be a loan officer, I didn't even know what that was. But it became my new dream once I learned. It's okay to change the plan, change the dream, take a detour or a left turn. Just don't stop dreaming! Don't stop doing. Don't stop learning. Don't stop showing up for yourself!

If your dreams don't scare you, they're not big enough

Chapter 3

Moms have Dreams Too

Raising a boy is basically feeding them nuggets and pizza and begging them to shower.

I know all my boy moms out there feel me! Literally, no lies. I actually read this quote on social media once and felt relieved after reading it. I truly want the best for everyone, but once I learn someone is going through the same thing I am going through, I feel normal and validated. I feel like I'm not in this alone. Sis you are not alone!

Right now, I have a son under the age of 10. We will just call him Noah. Noah enjoys reading, football, basketball and hanging with his friends. He wants to be in the NFL or NBA when he grows up. Shocker right. Don't we all want to be rich! I don't crush these dreams at all. I'm actually hoping and praying I birthed a star! He also loves the beach, video games and says he wants to be a YouTuber as well. So ambitious just like his mother.

Being a mom is the hardest thing in my life. I want you to re-read that. Being a mom is the HARDEST thing in my life. I know you can agree. We have to feed them, shelter them, play with them, make sure they are smart and confident. Make sure he has a bed to sleep in and nice clothes to wear. If you are not a mom and you are reading this saying all that is easy, basic stuff. Think again babe. Everything little single thing you do, just imagine doing it for someone else. Everything single little thing. I started carrying lotion in the car because sometimes I forget to make sure he not ashy before we the leave the house! Yes sis, every little thing! We have to teach them respect, math, reading, and all about God. Teaching them to fight and protect themselves, especially when you are not there to help. Hoping you've done a good enough job to make sure he is comfortable telling you if something bad happened to him. Make sure he has manners at the stores and other people's houses. Make sure he gets to see his friends outside of school, take him to church, sign him up for sports and so much more. We constantly worry about them when they are away. The constant fear of something terrible happening to the thing you love most in this world. There's so much pressure. Oh, and don't let him do something wrong at someone's house or in public. Now, we are bad moms, or we have a bad kid, or we don't know what we're doing, or "she doesn't have control of her kid". It's physically and mentally draining. Sometimes I literally want to run away and disappear. I've had some pretty dark thoughts regarding escaping the stress of raising a whole human being. I know you feel me.

I no longer question runaway mothers, drug addicts and alcoholics, because I get it now! I need a drink sometimes to deal with all the fear, the worrying, the questions, all the yelling and jumping and the extra housework. Literally one day I was sad for some reason and I went to the closet, closed the door and was crying for less than one minute and my son came in there asking me to help him with something. Like dang we don't even have time to cry! Sometimes I would rather be stuck in the back of the scary white van, y'all know what van I'm talking about. Sometimes I rather be in that van than have to deal with the pressure and responsibly of being responsible for someone else. I enjoy life but sometimes jail or being kidnapped sounds better than motherhood. A place where I just sit down and be still, don't have to do nothing else. Please tell me you feel me.

On the flip side it's the hugest blessing God could have ever done for me. For us. If you didn't feel me before, I know you feel me now. No matter what stress or happiness having children has bought to you, I know for sure we all are so very grateful that we have them. My son is the reason I am who I am today, my son is the reason I save money and try to be such this great person for. My son is the reason I am alive today. He gives me reason to want to be here on this earth. His voice makes me happy. His face brightening up when I give him any sort of attention. His smile gives me hope, it makes me feel like "Everything's going to be okay, you got this". When I put him in nice clothes and his hair looks good and moisturized and he looks and feels happy, I feel accomplished. And the fact he is a star at football and basketball, makes me feel like I birthed a professional ball player. All moms probably feel this way. I guess we just wait and see.

Co-parenting helps too. My son sees his father mostly on weekends, holidays, summers. The good part about co-parenting is that you get a break from your child. Whereas married people are with their children much more. Or shall I say most married people? Anyways—getting back on track! Although I need breaks from motherhood duties, when he is away, sometimes I feel so empty and sad. One day I remember I started walking to my room, then I walked to the living room, then back to room. I felt like I had no purpose. Just walking around the house looking for something to do. There's no reason to cook, or even be in the living room. On the bright side, we get to use that time to work on goals, go to gym, hang and party with friends. Or take a bubble bath and journal in peace.

The Single Parent Journey

Although my son's father is in my son's life, which I am so grateful for, I am a single mom financially and I'm a single mom when it comes to getting things done. I'm sure a lot of moms reading this can agree. We are the ones taking them to school, tutoring, school events, sports, activities, friends' houses, and such. We are the ones that plans, pays and set up birthday parties. We are the ones searching high and low for extracurricular activities and paying for them, after school programs and such. We are the ones that takes them to get their hair done and keep up with upkeep and try to keep them looking decent. We are the ones taking them to doctor and dentist appointments. Those dentist and doctor bills come to us. We the tooth fairy, we Santa Clause and so much more. The school calling us if there's a problem. We shelling out lunch money and helping with fundraisers. We are the parent that helps with homework and making sure the kids passing. Let's not use "that's a mothers job" or "that's what women do" as an excuse. Most of us moms not the weekend parent. We got the real part of the job and let me tell you something sis, you are doing amazing! Look at you, look at your kid(s). You got this! It's stressful and overwhelming for sure, especially during COVID, but we making it through. I know the kid(s) might have some stress, because that's life, but I know you're doing everything you can to make sure the kids are happy, healthy and safe. This may sound selfish, but on my son's birthday, I quietly cheers to myself for making it this far.

I can't go that weekend bro, I have my kid(s) that weekend.

-Said no man ever.

I understand the pain, frustration and loneliness of a single mom. You look up and it seems like everyone else around you has help and it makes you feel isolated and lonely._Women are too scared to divorce their cheating husbands because of the fear of the single motherhood journey and among other reasons I'm sure. Raising children alone, is probably at the top of the list for not leaving. Some women want the help so bad, they just get any man to play the father role to their children. Someone told me, a pastor actually, that the person that has a child and doesn't take care of that child will always be unlucky. I now understand why God keeps blessing me because I'm taking care of my responsibilities doing what I'm supposed to.

I talked about productivity throughout this book, and sometimes when I would get down and discouraged and don't feel like doing anything, or can't find the strength, I had to realize, once again, I'm not lazy, I'm tired. I'm tired of being two for one. I'm tired of being strong, being the backbone. I'm am tired of not even having the time to cry because I have to wrap a Band-Aid on him or start dinner then take him to practice. So, to all my single mothers and single parents with big dreams out there, I want to tell you, stop calling yourself lazy, you tired baby.

Now, with all that being said, I want to give a huge shout out to my support system. I am so grateful for my mom who helps me, my stepfather is actively involved and loves his Noah, my cousin will drop whatever she's doing to help me and for her I'm so thankful. My best friend helps and my neighbor who we are now friends helps. It helps that she has a son too, we just take turns watching the kids while we run errands or go on dates. My cousin, who recently moved down the street, now we help each other too. It does take a village, and I am so very grateful for mine, but you have to find and or build your village. And sometimes that can take a while.

Although, I'm the parent with true responsibilities, there are truly full-time single mothers out there who don't have a support system like I do, children's fathers are nowhere present. Dead or alive. This is why it's very important for me not to sit here and tell you, life is so hard and boo hoo, because I know at the end of the day, someone has it worse than me.

Forgive yourself

Forgive yourself for becoming a single mother babe. If you did not choose to, that is. Most of us dream about being a mother pretty much our whole lives. I know you didn't dream of doing it alone sis. We are in such a rush to make that dream come true that we can't even wait to mature enough to know what it means to build a family. To build a solid foundation with someone. Or to even build ourselves first, then to add children. We are also influenced by the outside world to have children while we are young, so don't beat yourself up for doing so.

I was sitting up watching Shark Tank one day, where a man was explaining the passion for his company and he said, with tears in his eyes, that his life changed the day his daughter was born. I was crying right along with him. This ambitious man on national television, doing whatever it takes, hustling, getting money to support his family. I thought to myself, why couldn't I be smart enough to have a baby with an ambitious man who values family. I know I'm not the only one thinking this. We can come up with 100 reasons of where we went wrong, and how we could have done better. I would question so many things. I didn't start meeting men that I was attracted to mentally until

I started maturing myself. I read a lot and now I know all the red flags. I beat myself up for not knowing at 20 years old what those red flags would have been. I beat myself up for not reading books about marriage and how to choose the right partner earlier in life. I wasn't thinking about that at 20 years old. As I'm sure you weren't either. I'm in such a better headspace, that I can laugh about this now, I got quite a few jokes actually, but the tears still flow from time to time. Forgiving yourself is something that's constant. There are days things may happen and we are upset all over again and those feelings of regret start coming back, but we have to catch ourselves. Remind ourselves that we bought a beautiful amazing child into the world and although things can be better, our child(ren) are perfect. Yes, babe, perfect. Your child is perfect! Period.

I have a birdie in my ear that tries to encourage me and say "you didn't know this would happen". There's no way to be sure of what type of parent your spouse would be to your child. Even if that person has other children, whether they are there for their other children or not, we all hope that with us, it will be different, but we can never guarantee. I hated myself for years for being another broken family. For being another statistic. There's also no way to know if you will stay with your child's father or mother and parent them together forever, even if you are married. We can't tell the future, be gentle with yourself.

This is my chance to tell all single parents that desire more for their kids, that you didn't know better. When we know better, we do better. Forgiving myself is a process and it took years to even get to where I'm at mentally with parenthood. First, I needed to realize that I need to start that healing process. Every year on my child's birthday the single mother journey really triggers me because if I don't plan and or pay for a party, my son's birthday would not celebrated. Find out which part of the journey triggers you so that you can control your emotions in that moment. Everyday isn't rainbows and bunnies, forgiveness is a journey. I'm honestly still working on this but you have to forgive yourself for you sis. For the happiness of your baby, your child, for the peace of your household. People love to say Happy Wife, Happy Life. Well single parents matter too. On both sides. Single moms and single dads. Happy Mommy, Happy Children. Happy Daddy, Happy Children.

Kids keep us going. That's the best part about having them around. There's no time for sadness. "What's for dinner" "My tooth hurts" "What are we doing today" "Can come Maxwell come over". As Abby Miller would say, *"Save your tears for the pillow"* We have a job to do!

Confidence in the child

One of the hardest things about parenthood for me is making sure my child is confident. I notice he is kind of like me, once I get to know a person, then I will open up. My son is the same way. I do feel like my son struggles with confidence. He is still young, I understand this, but it all starts now! We as parents must tackle this now so it can get better not worse. We are going to talk about ways I think can help our children be more confident and what's working for me.

I feel responsible for my son's self-esteem. Like it's my job to make sure he knows and feels like he is smart, handsome and that he can do anything. If someone is being mean to him and calling him names, I don't want him to take it personally. If someone is making fun of his hair or anything about him, I teach him that people will talk about you no matter what. You have to love yourself so much that you don't care what they say! Yes, I teach my child to say "I love myself". You should too sis. I teach him to take up for himself. We actually do role play, which is pretty entertaining and I'll pretend to be a bully and teach him to stand up for himself, or listen to see how he would. If someone calls him an idiot, because I see kids love that word, I tell him to tell that person he isn't an idiot and to please do not say that. I want him to feel confident speaking up for himself. Even when it comes to me. Back in my day growing up, we were not allowed to talk back to our parents whatsoever. I do feel like this creates timidness into adulthood and then you start letting people talk to you any kind of way. At least, that's what happened to me. I don't want my son to feel like he can't express himself. If I say something to him he doesn't like, or that hurts his feelings, or even when he is telling me a story and I don't believe him, I want him to be able to express himself. Respectfully express himself. I notice that whenever Noah wants to express himself he'll say "excuse me mom, can I tell you something" all shy, smiling and swinging his arms side to side, "you hurt my feelings earlier when you said blah blah blah." I'm now looking him in his eyes to let him know that I care and that I'm listening. We talk about it and I apologize. Yes, I apologize to my son all the time.

Yes, you can apologize to children. Sis, we make mistakes too. It's okay to model the behavior we want to teach our kids. We teach children to respect us but I realize some adults don't respect kids. Recognize your child's feelings too. Let's recognize when we are wrong and say sorry. Be an example. I expect my son to use his manners, therefor I will practice what I preach by showing him how manners are used. I say 'excuse me' to my son, 'bless you', 'I'm sorry', 'I didn't mean that'. There are times I snap at my son and if I don't apologize in that moment, I come back around later to apologize with no shame. Be a leader. Show your child that you know you are wrong too sometimes. Explain why you are sorry or why you snapped or yelled or whatever you did. This teaches your child that you recognize their feelings as well. Which gives them confidence. Now they feel like Mommy loves me again. She isn't mad anymore.

Another thing I feel like can build a child's confidence is creating a prize for being good. Weather its money, like an allowance, or letting a friend come over or letting them play on the tablet a little longer. I know some parents have a weekly chart for the kids and they can check off when they did their homework and chores to get a prize for the week. I haven't adopted that yet, which I intend to, but my son is pretty good without all that stuff. I kind of feel like that's more for children with siblings. I will say, if your child is struggling with confidence, I do feel like it would help because when checking things off a chart saying you completed it, makes anyone feel good, even us as adults. We all like feeling proud of things we can get done.

Another thing I try to do to help my child be confident is praying together. I want him to have a relationship with God. Having a relationship with God can provide a sense of security. When you need to talk to someone, sometimes you just want to talk to God. Most kids nowadays may not do this, but I was introduced to God at the age of four, and till this day we have a strong, amazing relationship. I talk to God when I'm feeling happy or down and I want to instill this behavior in my son. It's so important to be able to call on a higher power for personal guidance.

Another way to help our children with confidence is simply to praise them. "that's a great idea!" "Wow, thanks for helping me today" "I really appreciate when you did xyz". Thank them for helping you.

"Thanks for taking out the trash, such a strong young man!" Just like we have to stroke the male ego, we have to boost our children up too! These are simple ways to help your child feel more confident. You'll start to notice a smile, or that they are helping more or trying harder at something because they are waiting for that praise from you. We all want our parents' approval right! Even when you become an adult, low key, you still seek your parents' approval (most of us).

Simply giving your child attention gives them confidence. Let's put the phones down and watch your child do something cool. When they are trying to show you something, be attentive. Watch a movie or TV with them and show them you care about the things they care about. Play games with them like Charades or Pictionary. My son loves when I play with him or simply watch him play. He wants me to see him making his basketball shots or winning first place in Mario Kart. Let them help in the kitchen. My sons first time cracking an egg, the biggest smile on his face made cooking fun again. He likes to make cookies and brownies of course. So the fact that he knows how to go in the kitchen and make something builds his confidence. Like *yeah, I can cook like adults*. Let's be honest, kids like being independent. It's an ego booster. Be there for them. When they say they are scared of the monsters in the closet, recognize their feelings and do something about it. Instead of the famous "monsters aren't real" talk, just try to relate to them and tell them how you felt as a kid or what you did when you were scared of monsters. Or be like me and pretend to fight the monsters by getting the nerf gun or using my famous cheerleader kick to pretend to threaten them if they come in his room. And then of course I do tell him they aren't real. But I want him to know if something is in his room, Mommy to the rescue!

Talk nicely to your child(ren). When we talk nice to our children, instead of yelling all the time, it can give them an easy feeling. I used to be a yeller and I feel like that had an impact of his confidence. In fact, I know for sure that had an impact on his confidence. I'm not saying I would yell all day, every day, but I found myself yelling at least once or twice a week and I didn't like it. I would yell mostly because I was frustrated. I was mainly frustrated because I always felt like I was doing this on my own, tired or burnt out. Like being mad at myself for being a single mom. I had to realize my son didn't ask to be here and don't take my frustrations out on him. These times were the times I would apologize to him and let him know why I yelled. I also felt like a bully and knew I needed to change my behavior. Besides that, that's how I see other people parenting their kids, so I thought that was the way. I hate the look in his eye when I would yell. But I will say, I love how he still felt confident enough to tell me he doesn't like being yelled at. That a strong, bold kid right there. I respect that. Honestly, I don't like being yelled at either, so why would a child like it. I'm no longer a yeller. I mean, well the time he dropped my laptop on the floor with this book draft in it, I definitely yelled. Now of course we all yell sometimes, especially if they break a lamp or ceiling fan wing! Oh yea, he broke my other ceiling fan wing playing basketball in the house. I didn't care, so I didn't yell but honestly, I should have. So now we only have two wings on a four-wing ceiling fan. That definitely would have been the time to yell. Now I know we all yell at our kids, especially those with teenagers sneaking out the house and sneaking the car out. I'm not saying don't yell at your child. I'm trying to say, don't make yelling a form of communication. I mean, unless you just have a rebellious child, you may want to seek counseling. Let's stop the generational yelling and talk to our kids. Love them, guide them, show them what's right or why that was wrong. Now that I'm wiser, I'm more accepting of my life and my journey and focused on staying in my feminine energy and now I barely yell. I don't have the energy. I had to realize he is child, he doesn't know things, he is looking for my guidance, my help, my leadership. Our children are looking up to us, we are the leader, their God or higher power, they seek our approval, they are waiting on our instructions. Guide the way in a healthy loving way that makes them feel good about coming to you for anything. Effectively communicate by just simply talking and or telling them why this and that is wrong and what could be done next time.

Also, don't just sign your kid up for stuff. Excel at it. Encourage confidence by pushing your kid to be the best so they can win all the awards at the end of the season, or the show, whatever it is. I signed my son up for Boy Scouts just to have something to do. They had a fundraiser happening that I had no intention of doing. Not at all sis. Then I thought to myself, that energy right there is what will make my son average. I don't want him to be average. I want him to be the best at everything he does. I want him bringing home trophies and awards. We had 9 days left to sell popcorn and we sold over $500 worth of popcorn and he ended up being top salesman in his age group. Encourage them to practice more, to be better, watch videos and read about someone that inspires them. I watched my son line up in sports and I saw he was always last in line. I have little talks with him to try to boost his confidence so he can be first in line. Not last. We want the kids in the front, not the back! Just like we want to be first, or on top, let's get that energy in our kids. It also teaches them that we won't win every time, how to handle not winning and that you are still enough when you don't win something. You see what I'm saying?

My dreams Matter

"Let me put my glasses on and get this map out. Can somebody point me to this village everybody talking about!?" Inside joke with my favorite person.

"It takes a village" they say. It takes a while to build this village, but once you have it, a solid one, don't do anything to jeopardize it. Sometimes having children makes you feel like you can't do what you want to do. Especially when they are young, it is an obstacle, I will say. However, every time I feel like I can't follow my dreams and be a mom at the same time, I think of all the moms that are graduating college, and or starting businesses. They are my real inspiration.

I used to feel like I couldn't get much done with my son around. We go to work, come home, cook and play and I would try to muster up the energy to edit a video, study or do whatever it was I was trying to do at the time. As he got older, it got easier. He can now play and entertain himself while I work on my projects. Sometimes he even helps me with my projects. He's a great photographer. Now I just have to teach him how to record me properly. The point is, don't let your kid stop you. You can even teach them how to help you and make it fun. Sometimes I do still need to find a sitter if my project is more complex or involves multiple people. I've been in a few music videos for local rappers and I definitely found a babysitter for those projects. Don't let you kids make you feel like you can't follow your dreams.

I encourage you to take the opportunity of letting your village help you. Tell them your dreams or what you're trying to accomplish and see who can help out with babysitting or in other ways you might need help. I mentioned getting a nanny or babysitter if you can. I sometimes pay my friends to watch my son that way they don't feel used. Everyone likes to get paid right? If you can, show some appreciation every now and again, by taking them out for dinner or drinks or buying a gift. Whatever you do, never let your kids be the reason you don't follow your dreams. Don't be afraid to ask for help.

Affirmations for Single Parents

- *I let go of blame*

- *I am a great parent*

- *Now that I know better, I'll do better*

- *It's okay to ask for help*

- *I am more than a "single parent"*

- *My past does not define me*

- *My dreams matter*

- *I am allowed to feel the way I feel*

- *My child is love and feels loved*

- *I find time to have a social life*

- *Its okay to have a social life*

- *I am confident in my parenting skills*

- *Parenthood looks good on me*

- *My self-care matters too*

- *I feel calm under pressure.*

- *I am open to learn new parenting skills*

- *I am a great role model*

- *I will not compare myself to other parents*

- *I will not compare my child to other children*

- *Pain is temporary*

Chapter 4

Goal Digger

"Girl, he don't even have no 5 years goals or nothing, don't know what's next in life and can't even keep a job".

I was on the phone gossiping one day with an older friend of mine who was talking about an older gentleman. How she was fed up with him. Honestly, the only thing I remember from that conversation was her saying he didn't have five-year goals. I thought to myself, *I don't even have five-year goals.* I was at Corner Bakery enjoying some lunch that day and I immediately went home after I finished my meal and began to write down everything I wanted to do in life. Anything I wanted to accomplish, everything in my wildest imagination and just started writing. Planning and organizing. Every Cosmopolitan and Women's Health magazine had my money that month. I started cutting out pictures, using the work printer to print off images from Google of things I wanted in life and next thing I know I had a vision board.

I created a vision board in 2018 and literally did EVERYTHING I said I was going to do. I was introduced to having five-year goals. 2018-2022. I had no idea how I was going to do any of it, I just had a vision and at least wanted to try! Some things just happened. I have a quote on there that says "work from home". COVID happened, and now I done messed around and manifested working from home. Does it matter how it happened? No!! It happened. We always down play ourselves and say "that doesn't count", honey, yes it does. It happened and here we are. Same thing with the traveling-I didn't realize I would travel so much. I had a picture on my board that said "travel like a boss" and now guess what? I'm traveling like a boss. I even bought a suitcase one day because it was on sale, before I started traveling frequently. Next thing I knew, that suitcase always found its way to the airport. I truly believe I manifested my current life by creating that board. Goal accomplished! Vision boards can help you see the vision, even virtual boards like Pinterest or something on your phone. Just write it down or make something with photos so you can look at it all the time and constantly manifest.

Now we are going to discuss goals, how to map them out to actually get it done.

I highly suggest writing down everything in life you want to accomplish and most importantly, place a date on it. You also want to incorporate things from your mission statement. For example, I to strive to be fit and eat healthy. I strive to volunteer and or donate to a charity. Make sure when you're writing out your goals, you are incorporating them with your mission statement and placing everything you want to do and everything you want to be down on paper.

I feel like when people hear the word goals, they think of money. Remember goals don't always have to be about making money. You can have a goal that you want to stop cursing, become sober, get in shape, or learn a new language. There are so many types of goals. There are fitness goals, work goals, family goals, personal goals, money goals, hair goals, the list goes on. I have over 25 personal goals and only 5 of them have to do with money. If you don't have goals, that's ok. Hopefully by the end of this chapter you will realize that you may actually have a goal but didn't look at it as a goal. Or can come up with a goal or two. Be gentle with yourself.

At work, most of us have daily production goals. Apply that same energy to your life sis. Make daily goals, even if the goal is to rest on Sundays, that's still a valid goal. God himself, wants us to rest on the Sabbath Day. You need rest. Have daily, weekly, monthly, quarterly, and yearly goals just like a business does. Your life is your business. You are the CEO.

I'll walk you through a day as a loan officer just to give an example of how we run our lives at work and can apply the same principles to our personal life. Bear with me, sis. At work, I have a list of things I do daily, I call it my *daily formula*. My goal at work is fund 11+ loans a month in order to make 5 figures a month. To get there, I have to do my formula daily. That formula is to get 4-5 credit pulls which means I've talked to 4-5 people today that actually qualify for a mortgage loan, 2 Pre-approvals, meaning that I've approved at least 2 people today that I've previously talked to. 15+ outbounds a day meaning I'm calling and following up with my current pipeline of clients, checking in on them seeing if they found a house yet. This is my personal daily formula. Or course sometimes we may not accomplish the goal every single day, but you must definitely have a goal or a vision.

Monthly goals at work include 60+ credit apps, 30+ pre-approvals/ month, 14+ locks, 11 fundings- if I do this monthly I can possibly fund 11+ loans a month. No, these numbers don't add up, but these are the goals. Again, bear with me. Now some loans fall through and don't get approved, that's why you want to lock 14 or more, in case 3 don't go through, you still fund at least 11 loans.

Those are work goals. Think about your goals at work and see if you can apply the formula to your personal life. Basically, replace the work jargon with street talk. In my personal life I set weekly, monthly, quarterly, yearly and 3-5 year goals. Sometimes I fall off. I get tired or discouraged sometimes. However, I try not to fall off 2 weeks in a row.

If someone ask you what you want to be in 10 years, I would flip the question and ask them back. You'll find that most people don't know EXACTLY what they want in ten years. The obvious answer is to be rich and or retired, and if they give you that answer, you dive deeper and ask them how. Most people, don't know what they want in 10 years. Let's take it down 3 to 5 years at a time. That's more attainable.

If you give yourself 30 minutes to complete a task, it'll take you 30 minutes. If you give yourself 2 months to complete that same task, it'll take 2 months.

Let's start from the top. 5-year goals, where do you see yourself in 5 years? So now we break it down yearly. In year #1, you want to accomplish, let's just say learning a new skill and getting a certificate or a license or finish getting your degree. In this case we will say year #1 we want to obtain a real estate license. In year #2 you want to buy a house and travel out the county somewhere. In year #3 you want to buy a second home/beach home by add more money to your retirement. Year #4 you want to pay off some debt, own or buy a business and write a book and in year #5 you want to extend your family, whether that's getting married, having a kid, or another kid. These are examples.

So now we have our 5-year goals, feel free to do a 3year game plan if you can't see in 5 years just yet. Not everyone knows what they want in 5 years, some may not even 3. Remember, be gentle with yourself. So now we need to map out yearly what we want to accomplish to achieve our yearly goals.

Year #1- set a study schedule to achieve to finish school, or get that certificate. If you are doing something that doesn't take the full year like getting a real estate license, let's say you pass your test early in the year or mid-year, the rest of the year should be spent getting hired and building your book of business. You can even get a head start on some of your other goals. Check off one thing and move to the next.

We won't get into each year because you get the point by now. So now we have our yearly goals, we need to map out Quarterly what we want to accomplish to achieve our yearly goal.

Quarterly goals can look like the following:

Jan-March- Go to Real Estate School, get Real estate license. Hawaii for Spring Break, loose/gain 15 lbs. , save 10% of monthly income, read at least 3 books, kid(s) will do swim lessons and computer class, volunteer for charity or donate to a charity.

April- June- possibly still studying for Real Estate license, get license, loose another 15lbs, save 10% of monthly income, read at least 3 books, kid(s) will play basketball, volunteer for charity or donate to a charity.

July- September- Continue school- if you chose something that will take longer. Search for jobs, Family trip to Disney, save 10% of monthly income, read at least 3 books, kid(s) will play summer sports/activities, volunteer for charity or donate to a charity.

October- December- if you are behind on any goals, get caught up realistically. Real estate- get hired and build a book of business, volunteer for charity or donate, save 10% of monthly income, read at least 3 books, kid(s) will play football or whatever sports, finish the year losing another 10lbs (insert fitness goal here), start prepping for year #2 goals.

Monthly goals can look like: we are going to use year #2 for this section

January- read one book, save $xxx, take kid(s) to museum, gym 3x/week, kids doing swim lessons on Saturday mornings,

February- read one book, save $xxx, try a new restaurant for family night, gym 3x/ week, kids are still in swim lessons on Saturday mornings, file taxes

March- Spring Break vacation, decrease debt, volunteer for charity or donate, post a YouTube video (insert hobby here), read one book, gym 3x/week

April- kids are playing basketball, read one book, save $xxx, gym 3x/week

May- Read one book, save $xxx, gym 3x/week,

June- Summer vacation out the country, kids are doing summer reading program, volunteer for charity or donate, post a YouTube video, book of the month, save $xxx, gym 3x/week

July- kids are playing summer sports, read one book, save $xxx, gym 3x/week

August- read one book, save $xxx, gym 3x/week

September- volunteer for charity or donate, read one book, save $xxx, gym 3x/week

October- Buy lake/beach house (secondary property), read one book, save $xxx, gym 3x/week

November- post a YouTube Video, read one book, save $xxx, gym 3x/week

December- catch up on goals if behind, start setting up for next year's goals, volunteer for charity or donate, takes kids six flags/winter vacation, read one book, save $xxx, gym 3x/week

Everything is repetitive, just like a job, just like life. Most of us have the same daily routine. We go to work or school, come home, cook dinner, do homework, or extracurricular activities then it's time for bed. Weekends we see our family and friends, Sundays some go to church, it's all repetition. Some months may not be much going on and that's ok. You saw a lot of repetition in the monthly goals because we have to keep saving money, we have to keep going to the gym if we want to be fit, we have to keep studying if you want to achieve something. even when you get that dream job, or business, it's all repetition. Every year change the oil on the car, we file our taxes, we run our numbers and do our books. Even our bodies, we shower and wash our face daily. It's all repetition babe. Repetition.

As we discussed there are several types of goals. If you want to travel, write down the places you want to go and put a date on it. Be sure to look up when the best time to travel to the that city. For example, the best time to travel to Mexico if you want to see the beach with no seaweed, is around November-March. This is based off experience; I did not look this up. However, Travel.usnews.com says the best time to travel to Chicago is April through May and Sept- Oct. Also, depends on your goals when traveling. If you want to go skiing in Denver, you may want to do some research on when it will be snowing in Denver, sis. Don't do like I did and go in June when there is no snow. We had to redo the trip just to see some snow. No complaints though, always a good time with babes. So do your research and start placing dates on when to go places.

Travel Goals can look like:

Hawaii- Spring 2023

Disney- Summer 2023

Singapore- Spring 2024

Punta Cana- Fall 2025

Exercise goals can look like:

Monday- cardio, abs, back, buttocks-

Wednesday-cardio, abs, legs-

Saturday- cardio, arms, abs, buttocks

Or

January- March- lose 15 lbs, be able to run 1 mile

April-June- lose 15 lbs, be able to bench press 120lbs, be able to run 2 miles

July-September- Be able to do the splits, run 2.5 miles, bench press 150lbs

October-December- tell your story, help others accomplish their fitness goals

Placing a date on your goals helps you take action. If you know you have to get this done by Friday, it makes you put a move on things. If you know you want to go to Hawaii in Spring 2023, then we need start researching flights, hotels, excursions so that we know the average cost and can determine how much money we need to save for the trip. If you know you want your real estate license before summer, then you know you need start studying so you can be up and ready by summer. If you know you can afford a new car by next year if you save $xxx/month, then do the work, save the money and get that new car by such and such date. Slap a date on it! Slapping a date on it helps you determine how much you need to save monthly so you can get the car/item.

This may seem all over the place, I just wanted to give some examples, and also some repetitive stuff so you can see how being repetitive can make you successful (in most cases). Another reason It's important to write it down and check things off to make sure we don't suffer from burn out. Writing it down is basically mapping out what you want and when you think you can accomplish it. We mentioned exercise (insert your personal goals here) earlier in the book. So on your weekly goals; we need to add exercising to the routine. Remember, everything doesn't have to be so calculated, this is just a layout for the week. This is basically what we wish to accomplish and getting yourself mentally prepared. Even writing simple things down like what are we going to eat, can even help save money if you have it planned out. AKA meal prep, and there are books for that.

Weekly Goals can look like this:

Sunday: hanging with friends/family, deep cleaning the house, and/ or working on side hustle #2 6pm-10pm

Monday: gym 6am (before or after work), work 8-5, wash hair, (eating leftovers)

Tuesday: Kids tutoring 7:30am, work 8-5, basketball practice 6-7pm, side hustle #2 8-11pm ...keep in mind, basketball is a season. This isn't a permanent schedule. We all know the hustle and bustle of everyday life.

Wednesday: work 8-5, study Spanish on lunch, gym at 7-8pm

Thursday: Noah Tutoring 7:30am, Work 8-5, date night or family night (you can alternate date night biweekly and family night biweekly- just an idea), side hustle #2 8-11pm or after the date

Friday: work 8-5, study Spanish on lunch, rest night (during basketball season this is a practice day, practice 6-7)

Saturday: Study Spanish, gym/workout, kids sporting events (you can even workout at your kids games, it's called multitasking), family day like lake day- or some weeks just chilling, studying, catching up on goals

Daily goals can look like:

Morning affirmations

10-minute workout (minimum)

Study for 1 hour

In case you're wondering, well when do we eat. In my family we eat when dinner is ready. It doesn't matter what time something happens, just do it and get it done. Don't stress out because dinner isn't on the table at 6pm like on TV. Cook when you get a chance. I also work from home, so I mostly cook dinner during my lunch hour that way after work we can eat and get moving to the next things. So, it's all about your schedule and how you map out your life. If you have a spouse or partner, put them to work! While you are accomplishing all your goals, you can be alternating with your spouse on who cooks dinner.

This schedule can look intimating, but remember, some things are seasonal. Kids sports are seasonal, side hustle #2 will get easier as you get better or if your side hustle #2 is a second job, maybe one day you won't have to work that second job, if your side hustle #2 is writing a book, well you won't be writing forever. Some projects are seasonal. Don't get scared looking at the planner. Think of your projects timeframes as semesters in college. Sports are like 6-8 weeks out of the year. Your projects may be 2-3 months at time. Then give yourself breaks just like college. Also, you can alternate some things. Like maybe you only work on side hustle #2 every other week, or one weekend a month. Make the schedule fit your lifestyle. If you know you can only afford a babysitter once or twice a month to work on your side hustle or hobbies, then do that, that's okay. Remember, we are not comparing ourselves to others. We stay in our lane. Know what you are capable of. Some weeks may be busier than others, some weeks you might give yourself a break and just catch up the next week. This is all okay. Things happen, we get distracted or discouraged, or simply tired and drained. Schedule time for rest. My rest days are Friday nights. Every week- make sure you do something that your future self will thank you for.

Tip: Have an accountability partner. Tell someone you trust your goals and make them hold you accountable. One of my gym nights I go with a friend. This adds on pressure to go. If you have a date scheduled with someone, you don't want to cancel right? You want to show up for your friend or accountability partner and kind of prove to them that you are going to do what you said you was going to do. Having a partner helps so much. They can question you and make sure you are working on your goals.

We all fall off. We get tired, discouraged, and burned out. A phrase I love that Lilly Singh said in her book: "Expect it and address it". A huge mistake we make is waiting a long period of time to start over. If you have a plan to not have a drink for a week, and on day 4 you have a drink, you don't have to wait until Sunday or the beginning of the week to start over. Literally you should start over the very next day. The very next moment is the best time to try again. I promise you babe, you don't need to wait till the new year to start some new year goals. Do them now! Now is the best time.

Assignment- Write down at least 20 goals. All types of goals- saving money, exercising, growing your hair, expanding yourself more in your career, growing your business, spending more time with your child(ren), learning a new recipe, it can be anything! ...and remember, be gentle with yourself.

Chapter 5

Time Management

*I*nstead of listening to music while driving, cleaning, or doing your hair, you can listen to a podcast or something educational or meaningful.

The main question I get is how do you do it. "Nisha, how do you have a job, houses, a side hustle, how do you have money and time for vacation and travel. How do you do it all with Noah." Time management baby. I manage my time. Everyone is on a schedule. Even my "boyfriend". Just kidding but not kidding. I have certain days for gym, certain days for dates, certain days for hobbies. According to 16personalities.com My personality type is logistician. I'm very organized, and live with a sense of urgency. Everything is on a calendar. If you ask me today to go to a concert on November 12th, I'm putting it on my calendar that way I now have that time blocked off to spend with you. I even have the day I wash my hair scheduled. It's called "Wash day". My sistahs know what I'm talking about.

Time management is so important if you want to success in something. Anything. Most women are natural planners, for example, we can schedule a brunch and already know what's on the menu before we get there. I schedule my gym time, my learning time and time I spend with friends and family. Of course, not everything is calculated and planned, girl. Sometimes I'm spontaneous and I'll hit you up and come over and chill with you if I have nothing going on that day. Even if you are going through a season in your life where you have nothing going for yourself, you must schedule what you do throughout the day. For example, have a morning walk, schedule when you eat, just to make sure you are not over eating, schedule some exercise, time for a hobby or time with family. Having nothing to do, or no hobbies can lead to boredom and depression and sis I don't want you out here getting depressed because we have nothing going on. I've been there. I'm sure you have to. What I do, is try to make sure that most days I do something that my future self would thank me for. For example- writing this book.

For all my stay-at-home mom with kids, summer moms/dads, all my remote working friends- put them kids on a schedule so you can have time for rest or yourself. Personally, for me, having nothing to do makes me feel like, for lack of a better term, a bum. I need to be doing something.

If you fail to plan, you are planning to fail

- Benjamin Franklin

I have so many things I want to do and sometimes I wish I can spend the day with the likes of Rihanna, Michelle Obama, Orpha, Will Smith, Kylie Jenner just to name a few. Don't you? I mean who doesn't want to spend the day with Michelle Obama or Will Smith? I want to see how they manage their time. How is it that you have 2- 3 movies in one year, a makeup line, a you tube channel, touring, magazine covers, talk shows AND lip kits. Like how- how do you do it? I know they hire help, but these are also their ideas that they are putting in the works. If I had one wish, I just need to know the schedule, so I can apply it to my life. We all need this schedule. Like please share the secrets!

The first step, sis, is figuring out what you want. What do you want to be? How are you going to be this person? What will you do to be this person? The quote we just read- "Envision the women/person you want to become, act like her, speak like her, dress like her, study like her, exercise like her, embody her, think about her, eventually you will become her, you will be proud of her." That quote really stuck with me. Personally, I want to be fit, so therefore I need to exercise and eat right. I want to be smart, so I need to read books and learn vocabulary and continue to be reading, listening to podcast and making sure I'm always learning. Eventually I want to speak Spanish, which means I need to be studying the language. I want to be wife one day, so I have to practice not being so independent all the time, asking for help, being vulnerable, showing emotions, love, being nurturing, showing the person I care, telling them I care about them and etc. Whew that was a lot! No wonder I'm still single. Haha. I also want to make sure I give back to the community. Growing up we volunteered all the time and I want to make sure I keep that going. For years of my adulthood, I did not do this. I recently started back volunteering in

2020. If I couldn't make the event, I would donate to the event. Life gets busy, but don't forget to help others as well. If you don't have time to volunteer, make sure you find a charity that your passionate about and donate every once and a while.

I'll be open and give you guys a few things here I want to accomplish. These are the things I want to be.

For me, I want to be

1. Wife/Mom

2. Loan Officer /Day job

3. Landlord/Real Estate Investor

4. Youtuber or just showing up on social media

5. Business owner

Let me explain:

1. Wife and Mom- Family First. I'm a mom first. The reason I actually listed this on my list first is because it is who I am and what matters most, but also because it is something that I want to be. It's the first thing on my list because it's the most important. I dreamed about a family ever since I was 7 years old. I may not have a full family, but my son definitely counts. Also, writing it down helps me not forget what I'm after in life and what I'm trying to accomplish. I am already a mom, but I want the family unit and I'm open to having more children. I would love to give my son a sibling. Having this written down at top of list, helps me stay focused on the main goal.

2. Loan officer or day job (whatever you main or day job is). Having a job or earning an income, is very important. So basically,

family first, then work is next. Maybe one day I will replace this with a business or maybe for you this is already a business. Basically #2 is about earned income.

3. Landlord/investor- #3 is basically the side hustle. My side hustle is real estate investing. I want to always own at least 3- 5 houses creating wealth for myself.

4. You Tuber/Blogger- this is just a hobby of mine. I love recording and creating because it's a fun distraction from day-to-day life stressors. Having the channel keeps me creative. I've learned how to make and edit videos, market them, create flyers and ads online, I've learned how to take and edit photos like a professional, these are all things I never saw myself doing a few years ago. I'm not tech savvy but having my channel keeps me knowledgeable about YouTube and search engines. I love that I know how to do that now. Maybe I'll get a job in marketing one day. Keep the palate open.

5. Business owner- I say business owner because this can be anything. An online boutique, being a travel agent, paid gigs and so forth. This is basically side hustle #2 or maybe #3 for you. Which will be your 3rd source of income. (1. Job, 2. Side hustle #1, 3. Side hustle #2) Because we need more than one income, more than two really.

You should have 3 hobbies, one that pays you, one that keeps you in shape, one that keeps you creative

With all that said, now we have to figure out how to do all of this. For starters, our full-time job has set hours for the most part. If you don't have set hours, I would like to suggest setting some just to stay organized. For example, let's just say my hours are Monday-Friday 8-5pm somewhere along those lines. Next, we have to figure out when we are doing the other things we enjoy or need to get done. I also mentioned I want to be fit. So now we schedule some gym days. Saturday morning, Monday Morning and Wednesday night. These are examples- you can choose any day. This also goes along with how to set goals. We have YouTube- (insert your hobby)- Now we need to schedule some filming. Important factors go into filming or showing up on social media. Like how often do you want to post? Decide how often you want to post and go from there. You can schedule a content day where you are changing outfits and filming and making content for your channel or blog. For example, you can film, edit and create content the first two weekends of each month and the other two weekends you can spend that time with friends and family. You can make enough content for a week, or two or the whole month if you can. This way the rest or your time, you can spend on your other goals.

Family time- For example, for me, my son's basketball is three times a week. So everything else I want to do, I have to do it around these hours however, while he is at practice, I'm either reading a book, editing a video, exercising or something so I'm still following my dreams but I'm finding a way to be productive. Always be productive. Don't let your family/children stop you from following your own dreams. We also want to schedule dates, play dates, lake day, or movie night. We try to have movie night at least once or twice or month. Sometimes, I take Noah to the park after work, as I'm sure you do for your kid(s). Or schedule a good ole Klyde Warren day. (a famous park in Dallas, TX). A lot of times during the weekend, I just go to mom's house and chill with her. Out of all our goals and things we want to accomplish, don't forget about family sis, and quality time with the family.

Being a landlord/investor- For real estate investing, once you have it up and running, you may not have that much busy work in it. You can hire a property manager or do it yourself. If you buy good properties, your tenants shouldn't have many problems, which creates less work for you.

Business owner-which we haven't yet defined, but for the sake of the example, we will use writing this book for example. This is side hustle #2, (well 5 for me personally) but you get the point. We need to schedule some writing time. Remember Monday-Friday 8-5 is already busy. Saturday morning, Monday morning and Wednesday nights we are at the gym. So what time do we have left? Let's say we are going to write on Sundays, Tuesdays and Thursdays. Be specific. Plan a time for writing (insert your hobby/hustle here). So Sunday night 6pm-10pm, Tuesday and Thursday night from 8pm-11pm this is side hustle #2's schedule. Remember this is a seasonal project. This is not your life long schedule so don't get intimated here. Make a goal to have this completed in six months for example and then work on promoting, selling and so forth. The hard part is over, which was writing. Now you have to sell. You can sell all day everyday by talking to people at work, sending text and emails and sending them links, or promoting on social media.

We must maximize our time. I saw a YouTube video about being a loan officer, the guy was driving in his car, had the camera propped up on his window, filming a video letting us know how to be a loan officer. He maximized his time. He figured, I can teach ppl while driving, while he's heading to his next appointment or where ever, he is following one of his other dreams. He probably has a family to get to after work and squeezed YouTube in when he can. You can use a calendar to stay organized, I use a planner, google calendar and the alarm on my phone. My closest friends laugh at me because I have so many alarms going off on my phone. It may get annoying and overwhelming, but I'm a boss babe. I want success, I like being organized, so these are the things that's need to happen. Even when I'm traveling, I'm maximizing my time. On long vacations you may can sleep in, but traveling and vacation is different. If it is a weekend trip like Nashville, Mexico or Arizona, a city that there's a lot of walking and so much to see, let's wake up because we have goals! I'm waking up early so I can go see the city, the beach in the morning while it's not so hot and crowded. I'm trying to see and get all my Instagram pictures where no one is all in my photos. I'm up early 9am sometimes 8, one time I was up at 7:30am to get to Paradise point in St Thomas. I wanted to see that view, and I made it happen. I'll sleep when I get on the plane or at home.

I also mentioned I want to learn Spanish. (Insert another one of your goals here- I am just giving you an example). I created a schedule and a goal of how I want to learn the language. I now take the time to learn Spanish 3x week for at least an hour each day. For example- class is Saturday before or after my workout, Wednesdays and Fridays during lunch hour. Each time I study, I just study for one hour a day. In my free time I make sure I'm studying my new words I learned for that week. I need to study at least 3x a week outside the actual class (that I made up on my own, which basically consists of a YouTube channel I found that teaches the language and have weekly courses for free). Again, insert your hobby or goal here and include it in the schedule. If you see me in the streets, don't ask me to say anything in Spanish! Just kidding.

Most nights before I go to bed, I try to do something for an hour that will help my future or keep me productive. You can do the same sis. That could be reading, or listening to an audio book, podcast, or studying something. Don't just exist in this world. Strive for better, aim higher! You are a queen. You are talented and once you get organized, we can see how to use your talents better and possibly turn yourself into a money-making machine. Or the best mom, or the best whatever it is you are trying to accomplish. I use my planner to keep me on point weekly with what I've done for the week so far. If I noticed I still haven't exercised for the week, (because we all fall off or maybe something came up), I'll squeeze in 100 sit ups and 60 squats. The fitness goal is flat stomach, nice buttocks right! So that quick workout is still productive towards my future. Aim to meet your weekly goals even if something on the schedule got cancelled because things happen right. Just reschedule it. My boo thing gets so upset with me when I cancel. He says you don't cancel; you reschedule. Apply that same energy to your goals. If you fall off, no worries. We all fall off. We get tired of having so much to do all the time. Just acknowledge it and get back to it! These are my tips on how to manage your time when you're working on different projects. I hope you find something useful in these chapters and use it towards your life. Always remember: Be gentle with yourself.

Stay organized, maximize your time and get on a schedule.

Chapter 6

Balancing Work and Life

Get a nanny.

I am totally messing with you!

If you want more out of this life, you probably hate being unproductive as well. Our minds are constantly running and we are constantly thinking about what we could be working on, and what's not being done. It's almost like we can't even watch TV without feeling guilty about not working on our goals at that moment or not playing with the kids. Watching TV and pretty much anything else at this point is a reward. If I work on project A and at least write for an hour, which is project B, I'll watch a movie or go out that night. I must feel productive before I do something unproductive. That's just me.

The previous chapter was about how to manage our goals in life. This chapter is about personal time away from goals and work. As a single working mom, I've learned how to use my lunch hour to get a lot of things done. Grocery shopping, waxes and self-care, running errands, buying stuff for the party, even cooking dinner. Girl, if you do this, by the time 6pm comes around, you have the rest of the day spend with family or work on some other goals. During sports season it's so productive because the kids can come home, maybe can eat or have whatever it is they needed for practice because you were able to get it on your lunch hour. Before the work from home era, I was still running errands on my lunch break, getting oil changes, gas and little stuff we have to do to maintain in life. I even go on lunch dates when I meet a nice guy. This way I don't have to find and pay a babysitter for evening dates. Just date while the kids are at school. Save money and find love! Win win!

I'm the type of person that beats myself up for not being productive. For wanting a nap, or for being tired. While everyone else has help, daily help, we over here working twice as hard trying to get small things done. We have to stop beating ourselves up for wanting a nap, or wanting a lazy day where we can lay down and watch a movie or two. Once again, even when it came to rest, I had to realize, I'm not lazy, I'm tired. So, before you put yourself down and call yourself lazy, think about everything you accomplished this week, or that day and stop beating yourself up. You're tired. We need help. God did not put us on this earth to do these things by ourselves.

Balancing is really important because we don't want to suffer from burnout. It seems like our generation preaches that "sleep is for the weak, you'll sleep when you die, if you are sleeping 8 hours a day, you'll be poor". This is simply not true. It's all about balance. If you can hire help, do it! That part wasn't really a joke. Life isn't about suffering. Even stay at home moms hire help, because it's just too much. They want us to cook, clean, birth children, bleed for almost 7 days, for current kids- play with the kids, help with homework, run them around the city for all their activities, look sexy for her man day and night and be a sex kitten. Oh, and do it all without an attitude. It's entirely too much, hire some help!

I love that the newer generation is promoting mental health, sleep, rest, downtime and hiring help. By any means am not I telling you to rest all the time and make sure you get your 8 hours of sleep each day. Let's be honest, we all want something more out of life- so if you are actually taking action on your dreams, you may not get that 8 hours of sleep each day. What I am promoting is a healthy amount of rest and me-time. Look at your schedule and see when you can rest and have those days to look forward to. My rest day is Friday nights. I get off work and do nothing. I've done all my cleaning, cooking, running errands, setting everything up to be able to rest this night. I did all the things for side hustles or any other projects, Sunday- Thursday, Friday, I just want to rest and sleep in Saturday morning. Unfortunately, my brain doesn't allow me to sleep in most Saturdays, because it's telling me to be at the gym, but you get my point. Find your rest day.

That's why time management is key. Time management helps us manage our time, place a date on the goals, and once you accomplish it, rest! Even if its something simple, get your rest in. Sometimes the reward is rest! Forget celebration dinners, let me get some sleep! Scheduling time to yourself is important, even if it means taking PTO from a job on a day the family won't be home- so you can have peace and quiet. This sounds silly but you should actually try it. Even if it's you and your husband switching days or hours around the house. Hey from 4-8pm, ask daddy, don't ask mommy, from 2-6 next day, ask Mommy don't ask Daddy. Switch days, help each other out. Assign the kids some chores to help you out. As I type this, I need to teach my son how to wash dishes so he can start helping. Right now, his chores are clean his room, clean the table, sweep and take the trash out. We haven't started with dishes yet. Anyways, sometimes when my son is gone, I just relax, sip champagne and watch tv. Sometimes I'll get a massage. I love chilling by a pool with a nice view or even some retail therapy. Shopping without my son is a whole different vibe. I get to take my time, try on clothes in peace and go to as many stores as I want! I'm getting carried away just thinking about it! Y'all know how it is!

Balancing comes to play here because most of us, when we are working, we are away from our children and families. I work from home so I really be wanting to go outside and enjoy other people any chance I get. I enjoy brunches and dinners with friends and a good day party like Sunday Funday. Somedays I want to go out and other days I just want to be "lazy" and write in my journal or watch TV. Let me tell you, sis, that's ok. It's okay to lay down and catch your breath. It's okay to not have plans today. It's okay to decline invitations. There will always be more. These are times when we can sit down and think. Think about anything, who we are, what we want to be, how you reacted to something the other day, how you can be a better person. We need time to think and plan. Before the COVID-19 shut down, I worked in the office and I drove to work. That 90-minute drive time a day was my time to think and plan. Sometimes I would listen to music, other times I rode in silence and just think. What I really miss about that time was praying. Let's be clear, I don't miss that drive at all, I miss the alone time I had. I talk about being productive and this is a time I am saying we must be productive. Whether its praying, phoning a friend you haven't spoke to in a while, listening to an audio book or podcast. The list goes on.

The past few chapters may sound busy and calculated, but remember, we are all human, we may fall off. In fact, we will. The key is noticing it, and getting back up and soon as you can, scheduling rest, asking for help or hiring help. For my people out here doing it alone, remember you aren't "lazy" you're tired. Get some rest.

Be gentle with yourself.

Chapter 7

Manage That Money Honey

Hey Girl, now I'm sure you are doing a great job, but we have to talk about this. I'm not here to tell you don't get your nails done and learn how to do your own hair. That's the first thing people try to take away from us when we talk about saving money. No mam. You are a woman and I want you to continue being a woman, whatever that means to you. Being a woman is expensive, no matter what upkeep it takes. We are going to talk about ways to manage our income, so that we can get our nails done, and keep them done! Or whatever it is that you don't want to give up that makes you, you, because you deserve it!

When I became a single mom, I had to cut back on a lot of things. I wasn't even getting my nails done at this time, I would paint them at home. Manicures and pedicures was nowhere in the budget back then. I cut off cable, switched my phone service from Sprint to Metro PCS. I even got a roommate. I even till this day rent books from the library because I'm still managing my money.

I taught myself early on how to spread $20 over one week. I was managing $20 allowance when I was a child, this is nothing new to me. My mom would give me $20 for lunch money each week. I went to the dollar store each week and bought $1 meals like noodles, canned fruit, mac & cheese and would save the other $10 for tumbling class. That didn't last long because I still can't tumble, but you get the point.

I did not want to ask my mom for more money, I worked with what I had and accomplished what I wanted. I got to eat and go to tumbling class. While everyone else was spending $5/day getting pizza, nachos and soda pop, I was actually saving my mom money. Mom, if you are reading, You're Welcome. Now that's love.

Now let's keep it real, we love to look good. They think it's cheap though. It cost a few hundred dollars to look, feel and smell this good honey. Between waxes, pedicures and getting our hair done is already $300+ a month. Skincare products alone is another $100+. Being a woman is very expensive but here's how I manage. Now that I do get manicures and pedicures, I decided I don't need a pedicure every time I step in the nail salon. Instead, I get a pedicure every *other* time. Just do a polish change most times. Let a pedicure be something special, like getting one before a vacation. This saves about $25. In the summertime we want to look good from head to toe since we are most likely showing more skin. So in the summertime I get waxed and during the winter or colder seasons, I'll just shave when necessary. Instead of going to the salon *all the time*, I just style my own hair. This saves me about $200-$300 a month. Or I invest in a really good wig that is long lasting and I take very good care of it, so that I don't have to get a new wig all the time. See how I'm not completely cutting off what makes me feel like a woman. We are just doing things in moderation.

Us ladies love a good cocktail when we go out to eat. Cocktails can range anywhere from $12-17 at most places where I live. While we are managing our money and cutting things out, we don't necessarily have to cut out everything we do, just try not to run up the bill while you're doing things you enjoy. Maybe instead of ordering 2-3 drinks and an appetizer when we go out, we can just order one drink. Just sip it slow sis. Sip it slow! Or skip the cocktails and get an appetizer. Or no cocktails, no appetizer and just get the meal. Or eat at home and just meet up for drinks. We have to find a way to make it work for the budget but still enjoy the things we do. I'm not just telling you to do it, girl, I currently do this too. I need to save as many coins as I can for the travel itch I be having.

Also, girl, do we really need the best phone service? We don't even answer the phone! Got these men on blocked, okay! Most of us paying over $100/month for a phone service but phone stay on Do Not Disturb. We rarely even check our voicemails. I'm not saying we don't deserve the best and I'm also not saying we have to go get a bad phone service, but maybe this is something we can think about when it comes to our bills. We don't need the best service every company has to offer. On some of my services, I have the basic plan and nothing is wrong with that. For example, on my gym membership I have the basic plan. I just want to simply use the gym equipment. I don't need the premium plan so I can play tennis. I know good and well I will never use that tennis court. See what I'm saying? Let's not over spend on the monthly stuff because those things add up.

I actually cancelled my Amazon prime because I only saved $40 in one year and I was paying $14/month. I would add things to my cart, and just keep adding until a bunch of items were there then I would click "order" so that I don't have a whole bunch of packages. I don't shop on amazon enough to get the benefit of prime, it did not make financial sense for me personally to have the Prime service. For us one income households out here, get with a friend and split the cost of a service you both use.

Let me tell you something sis, I have been working finance jobs since I was 19. My first finance job was doing payday loans. I would help customers that needed money till their next payday, paying high interest for a loan that they really couldn't afford to pay back. I would run their credit and see the report and see their other bills versus what their check was and I knew I never wanted that to be me. Even till this day, I'm still working jobs where I pull peoples credit and let me tell you- stop hating on people lives girl. We hating for no reason. Most people in America are living off credit. Stunting on Instagram with things they bought with credit, and in some cases not paying it back. I pulled credit for a guy once, his wife ran up over $70k in credit cards at Nordstroms, Macys and Rooms To Go and so forth and dude didn't even know it. She was really trying to keep up with the Joneses. I couldn't get him qualified because he, or should I say "they" had so much debt. When I pull these reports, I see people paying over $700/month for Toyota's and Hondas. That's a luxury car payment! We have to do better.

Now I know we all desire a life of luxury but until we get there, we must figure out how to manage the current income we have. We don't want to die tomorrow and leave our families with thousands of dollars of debt because we didn't manage our money well. We must decide on what's important in life right now with our current income. Which categories can we splurge on, and which categories we need to save on. For me, my category is travel. I want to see the world, and meet new and different people, I love the beach, I love snow, I love palm trees, I love the experiences travel give me. So, I will budget everywhere else in life so I can travel.

If you can't buy it twice, you can't afford it

- Jay Z

Part of money management is living within your means. I know it's hard to save money when everybody else is wearing designer. I know it's hard saving money while scrolling on social media looking at everybody going to Greece and Italy. This is another reason why it's important to take breaks from social media so that we are not constantly comparing ourselves to others or allowing the app to clutter our mind and become a distraction. Someone once said to me, I can't believe you drink Andre Champagne and you drive a Benz. What's wrong with Andre? If I can get something for $5 you better believe it's in the cart! Now if I'm celebrating something, I may buy a better brand depending on the crowd, but I love champagne and I enjoy a glass while watching TV. I don't want to waste a $60-$300+ bottle if I'm popping it by myself. That's no fun and its silly. Again, be smart. Where do we want your money to go, sis. Look at your vision board and remind yourself what your goals are so you can stay focused.

I'm no expert and I don't have a finance degree, I still work a 9-5 corporate job. So by no means am I trying to make it seem like I'm smarter, richer or better than anyone.

Below are some more tips on how to manage that money honey!

1. Anytime you get paid- pay YOURSELF first! Come up with a dollar amount or a percentage that you want to put away. For example, if your goal is to save $100/ month and you get paid bi-weekly, that's $50/check towards savings. You can even set up your direct deposit to where it splits into different accounts. This is the best way, that way you don't see it. This is how I save money for my son. It just goes in a separate account that I don't even pay attention to. Out of sight, out of mind.

2. If you are a homeowner, try to save at least 1% of the purchase price or value of the home, a year into your savings account. For example: if the home value is $250k, try to save at least $2500/year for home repairs. Which means save $208/month for the house.

3. If you are really ambitious, you want to set up a college fund for your child. Credit Unions have great accounts with competitive interest rates. Set a separate account for your child(ren). Set a dollar amount or percentage to save. For example, if you want to have $18k saved up by the time your child turns 18, then that's $1,000/ year, which means $83.83/month towards savings for 18 years. That's $41.66/check (if you are paid biweekly) towards your child's future. Doesn't that sound doable? You'll have that plus interest if you don't touch that money until it's time.

4. Cut the cable, cut the crap. Take a look at all the subscriptions that you don't use and look at getting a less expensive plan versus having the premium plan. Or better yet, girl call me so we can split this HBO Max and Audible!

5. Anytime you get a lumpsum of money, for example, a tax refund check, pay off debt, put the rest in savings. I promise this works! This way you keep debt low and still building your savings. All of this is counted towards our credit score. I try not to let my credit cards go over a certain amount every year. Every year when I get my tax refund, I pay my credit card(s) full balance and save the rest for a rainy day.

6. Don't max out your credit cards. I know we have so much going on baby girl, and everything cost money, but we need to

set a personal limit for how much we want to spend on our credit cards. Not the banks limit, a personal limit. Credit Karma and similar websites, recommend not to go over 30% of the limit. Once you've reach 30%, stop. Just stay at home! Tell them we will catch them at the next dinner party.

7. Create a saving account with a different bank than your checking account, this way you aren't constantly looking at how rich you are. (Speaking positive and manifest this money with me)

8. Get a savings account with high interest rates so you can earn interest on your current money. Credit Unions and smaller banks offer better rates than Bank of America's and Chase's .001%

9. Tell yourself that you are broke and keep saving and not spending money on silly items like Sprint $100 service and premium plans

10. Get Life Insurance

11. Don't tell people you have money.

12. Keep buying Starbucks!

I'm telling you girl, I enjoy shopping and eating out. That's why I say keep buying Starbucks or whatever it is you enjoy sis. Princess treatment only. There were times when I shouldn't have been spending money, I was still shopping and eating out. That's what I like to do. Notice I didn't tell you to stop buying things you enjoy. I know cable and expensive phone plans was on my list, but that's because it's silly.

Most people's biggest expense is probably the house payment. Forbes.com says your house payment should not exceed 28% of your gross income. I always lived in affordable apartments. It always seemed like everyone around me was paying four figures a month for rent while I would always find good apartments that were $700-850/month. I didn't stay in crap apartments either. They were 850-1100 sq feet units, I would always get 2 bedrooms and 2 baths. It was a nice, plain apartments, nothing fancy. No high rises in Dallas. I actually loved my apartments, they had pools, pool parties, free swim lessons and they always had family events. The fire station and police came by one day for the kids, and my 4-year-old got to step inside the fire truck, and they had Santa clause every year, and Halloween parties. My apartment complex was lit. One even had all new appliances. The point I'm making is, do more research. I refused to pay four figures a month for rent when I knew there was cheaper rent somewhere. I have a car note and a daycare bill, I have no choice but to live in affordable places.

The year I had a roommate, was the year I was able to put that money towards a dream and try to start something new. That was the year I actually started my YouTube Channel and was able to afford a new laptop, camera, software for video editing and the food for the channel. You see? Doing something that that my future self would thank me for. I had money to invest in myself, and buy the things I wanted for my hobbies and stress relievers.

The housing market is extremely crazy right now, but the point is, if you can, if at all possible, let's try to keep our housing payment under 28% of our income.

Don't pray for money, pray for wisdom

We must increase income. Think about all the money we have to save. We have to have an emergency fund in case there is a loss of income or a true emergency. We have to save for retirement. We are expected to save money for our children's college fund, if you are a homeowner, you have to save money for possible repairs. If you like to travel like me, we have our travel savings funds. The list can go on. Writing it all down is making me exhausted. This is the part of adulthood that we all hate, but let me tell you, I always had enough money to take care of myself and my son, I always found a way by the grace of God. Whether that was getting a roommate, a second job or becoming a surrogate mother, I found a way. This is the biggest confidence booster you can ever have. If you know you can bail yourself out of jail, or get fired, or something terrible happens and you can still take care of your family- there's nothing in the world that can stop you, that can scare you or make you feel inadequate. Money is one of the hugest securities you can have. I am highly aware that God can take everything from me have in a snap of a finger so I'm not trying to sound like I'm bragging here. I want you to *feel* what I'm saying when I say money is security babe. I highly recommend reading some finance books so we can educate ourselves and our spouses and families about how to manage what we have and possibly make more. Next, we are going to get into side hustles in different categories that I hope would be very helpful to you. I'll also be sharing some books I used to help me learn how to manage my money and build better money habits.

Like I said, you are doing great, but we can always learn how to be better. Be gentle with yourself.

Money Affirmations;

- *I am open to learn new ways to make money*

- *I am worthy of wealth*

- *I can provide my son a wealthy lifestyle full of the most fun memories*

- *I am open and ready to receive money now*

- *Money is attracted to me and needs me to spend it now*

- *Everything and everyone helps me prosper financially now*

- *Money flows into my life in large quantities through multiple sources now*

- *I am smart with money*

- *I am debt free*

- *Money makes me feel protected and secure*

- *My savings account is always growing*

Chapter 8

Side hustle ideas

Save your money! Save save save! That's all we ever hear. No one talks about earning more income. If you are a saver such as myself, there are no further steps then to keep saving. Well newsflash, its okay to spend your money. Yes, we just discussed how to manage our income, but the real key is to earn more. Not necessarily to spend more, but to thrive in life, not survive. We all want to afford the things we want in life without having to sacrifice too much, right?

I'm sure you've heard by now that most millionaires have at least seven streams of income. I challenge you, if you don't already to get at least three streams of income. Three honestly should be the minimum. I'm not talking about 3% cash back on a credit card. We're talking about actual sources of income. Our main job, sis, maybe one source is a talent like doing hair and/or lashes on the side and the 3rd source is being a notary or selling custom t-shirts or tumblers. These are examples. With the internet, there's no reason for us, yes sis, me and you, to not have another source of income. I asked for an iPad for Christmas because my goal with that iPad was to learn to make money online. I got the iPad, now my next challenge is to make money online. Let's tap into our talents and challenge ourselves.

I've worked 2 jobs like three times in my life, I've been paid to try products. There was a place called RCT up the street from my house, we would try new products and take surveys on them. Paying anywhere from $10-600. My friend did one that paid her $4000. I was never lucky enough to get that one but they are out there! I've donated plasma, I've sold detox tea, t-shirts and hats, I think I sold Avon products for like five minutes. Even became a surrogate mother. Yea, I know right. Girl, yes, I went to the extremes! Side Hustle is not only an income, but hopefully it's your passion. Having a side hustle will helps us determine what we like and don't like. Helps us determine how hard we are willing to work and whatnot. I'm the type of person that needs to be moving. When I sold my tea, I was going to events, setting up my stand and talking to people about their health. It was fun and I gained sales skills. Even though I don't make money from YouTube, I'm still learning and gaining a new skillset. Always stay learning my friends! I'm excited for the release of this book because it is my passion. Something I thought I would never find. Talking to people about my book is going to change my world. I'm ready to be traveling the world talking about my book. I will be online, pop-up shops, venues and more!

Don't know where to start? Well let's think. Do you find yourself complaining all the time or judging others? Be a movie critic, book critic, or magazine critic. Are you good at English and or love reading? Teach English, or edit people's books, or help them ghost write. Do you have a love for guns or a protective spirit? Be a bodyguard or security guard. Sign up to teach Licensed to Carry Classes. Work at a gun range part time. Are you good at making flyers, graphics and designing things online? Sign up on Fiverr and get paid for your talents! For all my men reading, are you a handy man? Good at fixing things around the house? Let people hire you to help them! I told you I hired a handy man myself. He had a business card with all things he specializes in. Do you have a nice voice? Do voice overs, or audio for books. Whatever your talent is, you can do it, or teach it. You can teach in person, at schools or churches or organizations, or online like YouTube or social media. Turn your talent into a side hustle. Doesn't even have to be a passion, if it can make you a dollar, do it!

Women have made side hustles seem easy! We out here doing hair, lashes, make up, nails. I honestly wish I would have caught the bandwagon for lashes. I have been to some very nice houses to get my lashes done. Like, ooh, this is what lashes buy!

I'm not here to tell you to take surveys online all day, however, some people do make great money for their opinion. I'm going to provide a list of ideas that I've come up with. Some of these ideas aren't even hustles, some of these are ways to save money. Some of it is earning another income and some of its spending money to get money in return, which is known as investing.

No is not an answer, It's an opportunity

- Jennifer Lopez

Here are a few more ways to save money:

- Rent a room out in your current home

- Rent your home out when you travel

- Get a roommate

- Refinance your home to lower the monthly payment

- File exemptions on your property taxes

- Do the points system at work to save money on your health insurance plan (every job has a way to save money on your benefits- do it and put more money in your pocket!)

Investing:

- Long Term Rental properties

- Short Term Rentals like Airbnb and VRBO

- Renting commercial properties out for parties/events

- Crowdfunding

- Angel investor/silent investor

- Investing in wine

- Dividends- (Fundrise is a crowd funding company that pays dividends)

- Stocks

Homeowners:

- Home Equity Line of Credit or Cash out refinance- this is not a hustle. This is borrowing money. However, a great idea if you have a business you want to start or buy.

Working and/or earning another income AKA side hustle ideas:

- Get a second job-literally- it's okay to work. Especially while we are young. Now, of course we want to find financial freedom, but in the meantime, until we can- lets go to work! There's nothing wrong with having a job.

- Rent your car out- if you have more than one car, you can rent one out, or rent them both out when you are not using one. Turo and Get Around are great platforms to rent out your car

- Rent out your watercraft sports- boats, jet skis, etc.

- Turn your car into an advertisement (get your car wrapped with advertisement and get paid while you drive. Carveritse.com)

- Design stuff and sell online- Etsy, Shopify, and Amazon. Example- t-shirts, jewelry, and tumblers.

- Sell a product on Amazon or Shopify- any product, doesn't have to be something your passionate about. People need batteries, especially during Christmas time, sell batteries or Valentine's Day teddy bears! Find a popular item and sell it.

- Learn about Drop shipping and start an online store

- YouTube, Tik Tok or social media- become an influencer

- Uber/ Lyft/Door Dash/Favor- things similar to this

- Food delivery service

- Personal shopper, secret shopper

- Affiliate marketing

- Tutor children k-12 or college if you can

- Interior design

- Get paid to try products

- Start a blog and promote it

- Detailing people's cars. (detail and wax)

- Be a ghost writer for books, music or poetry (if you are good at writing, poetry etc.)

- Write an E-book or a book

- Make low content books like journals, coloring books, activity books

- Become a copyright master

- Become a bookkeeper

- Join a MLM and sell a product (for example- I sold detox tea)

- Mount TV's on the wall for people who need help doing it

- Be a handy man

- Websites like Fiverr, Thumbtack, Angie's list- have a talent, post your talent online and get paid!

- Decorate, organize or clean people's homes and/or offices

- Manage or clean people's Airbnb properties.

- Become a virtual assistant or personal assistant

- Be a travel agent

- Real Estate Agent

- Property Appraiser

- Get paid to drive children to and from school

- Create a course online- teaching people to do something you are good at

- Be a secret shopper

- Become a notary and or loan signing agent

- Babysit! People still need sitters for a night out!

- Do makeup, hair, lashes

- Neighborly-rent out your garage for people looking for space/storage

- Be a voiceover- You can read audio books, do commercials

- Be an extra in movies- there are thousands of shows coming out and you could be an extra.

- Maybe a photographer/videographer- someone that even helps create the process.

Win Money-

- Play Poker

- Lottery

- Casino's

- Bingo and games to win money

- Win money playing games on the Radio

- Take surveys to win money off receipts from stores you shop at

Women that don't mind using your body to help others

- Become a surrogate mother

- Donate your eggs

These are some starter ideas and I hope they were helpful. Some of this stuff we've heard before but I'm hoping you seen something on the list that you haven't heard that may be a great idea for you. Or at least get you to thinking about your next step. We can also try furthering our education to learn more skills. Going to a community college to take a few courses, or even take an online course from your favorite blogger to learn something new. Google offers affordable courses to take for those of you looking to expand your knowledge and education. You can earn a certificate and start doing other types of jobs that pay more. Until then, EARN more income, using my time management skills that we discussed, if you have too much on your plate. Let's get this money, create these businesses and start generating more income for ourselves. If you can't get something started right away, that's okay. Maybe you can raise money or burrow money if you are serious about turning your side hustle into something bigger than your imagination but always remember, Be gentle with yourself.

Chapter 9

Recommended Reads

The first book I recommend reading is the Holy Bible.

Yes, I said it! Go read it, it's some good stuff in there. Scriptures we can all live by. Maybe you can find some scriptures that inspire you or keep you grounded when you about to pop off or simply need encouragement. I enjoy reading and, let me tell you, girl, it has changed my life tremendously. I want to share a list of books I have read that I feel have shaped me into who I am today. You may be wondering why I'm writing a book just to tell you to read other books. That's because I truly care about you. I believe you can change your life and the list of books I'm about to share, changed mine. It changed the way I view things, people and their ideology, money and more. These books can help in different categories of life such as work, life, love, and relationships with parents as you enter adulthood. These are books I have actually read and I'm sharing with you only my favorites. You may have heard of some of these books before. I would hate to sound redundant, but seriously, the set of books I'm about to share with you will change your life!

The books you read will change your life

Mindset and Character

The Four Agreements- Don Miguel Ruiz

48 Laws of Power- Robert Greene

Rich Dad Poor Dad – Robert Kiyosaki

7 Habits of Highly Effective People- Stephen R. Covey

Live Fearless- Sadie Robertson

Set Boundaries, Find Peach- Nedra Glover Tawwab

Emotional Intelligence- Travis Bradberry, Jean Greaves

Sacred Woman- Queen Afua

The Secret- Rhonda Byrne- This is actually a picture if you want to stream it on Amazon

40 Day Social Media Fast- Wendy Speake

Build Wealth

Get Good with Money – Tiffany Aliche

The book on Rental Property Investing- Brandon Turner

I Will Teach You to be Rich- Ramit Sethi

For the Certified Hustler

How to be Bawse- Lilly Singh

How to be a Boss B*tch – Christine Quinn

Women Who Work- Ivanka Trump

Parenthood:

The Confident Mom- Joyce Meyer

How to stop losing your sh*t with your kids- Carla Naumburg

For the singles

The Love Gap-Jenna Birch

Relationship Goals- Michael Todd

Getting to I Do - Sandra Harmon

Solving Single- G.L. Lambert

Men Don't Love Women Like You! - G.L. Lambert

Closing Statements

I really hope you enjoyed this read. I really enjoyed writing this for you guys. One of my top rules is to Protect your energy. I'm not saying have your guard up at all times, I am saying create healthy boundaries. That means saying "no" sometimes to the people you love. Putting yourself first. Removing all negative thoughts from your mind, removing all negative people from your space. Declutter your mind, meditate, focus on the positive. Take social media breaks this way you aren't constantly influenced by the outside world. Take breaks from negative people as well. You don't have to cut everyone off, just take breaks from them. Also, do not allow cell phones or even desperation make people think they have 24-hour access to you. Put that phone on Do Not Disturb and focus on yourself and your goals sis. You'll never regret it. Set some boundaries for yourself so that people don't invade or distract you from your purpose.

Remember, you can do whatever you want in this world with the right time management skills, the right people around you and the self-esteem you would need to make it happen. People say "Are you going to cry about it or are you going to do something about it". Well, first of all, I am going to do both, because I am a human with feelings. I am going to cry and do something about it. I may be crying while I'm doing something about it, and that's okay. Pain is temporary but it's still a valid feeling that you are allowed to feel.

Also, sis, let's all stop talking about our friends who are trying to start a business and just show some support. Whether that's buying their product or sharing their statuses on social media. Admire the hustle. Be encouraged. I love to see people trying new things to try to take their self or their families to the next level. People want to be so quick to talk mess about someone's business or say "Oh, I could have done that", well do it then! Let's grab an energy drink, quit sitting on the couch watching Netflix, drinking a beer, making excuses and talking mess and do something! Let's make moves, open the business, start that online shop or whatever it is. There are two types of people in this world. Talkers and Doers. Which one do you want to be? Always be a step ahead. A few steps if you can. **Stop talking and start taking action!**

Don't just do something, find a way to excel at it. There are doctors, lawyers, loan officers and regular workers like you and I, who have let the world know who they are and what they do. Let's say I make $250k at my job, but if I put online and let everyone know what I do, pass out business cards and network some more, I can make $310. Bring yourself more business babe. Don't be average. I tell this to myself too. Find something your passionate about so you can feel comfortable telling the world and possibly increasing your income. I have a cousin that is all over social media and the news selling healthy juices because that's her passion. Find that fire inside you and let the love and respect you have for yourself shine and inspire others.

I always tell myself **"life is as easy or as hard as I make it"**. Its true babe. There will be stressful times for sure but remember to find a reason to smile. Allow yourself to feel that stress but find ways to de-stress. I love exercising, so a good walk or a good stretch is a great de-stressor for me. Say your affirmations to yourself when you find yourself struggling. I struggled a lot emotionally and I would take a walk outside, sometimes with a coffee in my hand and just talk nice to myself. *I am strong, I am a great mom, I am a great role model, I am successful, I am capable of achieving this task.* You are too beautiful to be sitting up stressed and with an attitude. You are alive! You already winning right there. I love Kevin Harts idea of laugh at the pain. You can make it easy or you can make it hard. **You can choose stress or you can choose action and happiness.**

As I leave you, give yourself a hug for me. Give yourself more credit. You are doing an amazing job. There are people looking up to you sis. The book was a little repetitive but it's because I want you to know you are truly something special and I want to instill in your head. Or is it install it in your head? Just kidding. Be with those that encourage you. The ones that put you down, leave them where you met them. Let them watch you rise to the top sis. YOU ARE ENOUGH! PERIOD! Without begging for approval, without having to prove yourself, you are enough! I want you to be proud of yourself! Be proud of who you are! Be gentle with yourself!

Psalm 23 NIV version

The Lord is my shepherd, I shall not want

He makes me lie down in green pastures

He leads me besides the still waters

He restores my soul

He guides me in paths of righteousness for his name sake

Even though, I walk through the valley of the shadow of death

I will fear no evil, for you are with me

Your rod and your staff, they do comfort me

You prepare a table before me in the presence of my enemies

You anoint my head with oil, my cup runneth over

Surely, goodness, and mercy shall follow me

And I will dwell in the house of the lord

Forever.

Notes

Chapter 1:

<u>Www.BCC.com</u> https://www.bbc.com/future/article/20180104-is-social-media-bad-for-you-the-evidence-and-the-unknowns

www.WEBMD.COM -
<u>https://www.webmd.com/depression/news/20220506/one-week-social-media-break-reduces-anxiety-depression#:~:text=May%206%2C%202022%20--%20Taking,Cyberpsychology%2C%20Behavior%20and%20Social%20Networking</u>

Chapter 4

Travel.usnews.-
<u>https://travel.usnews.com/Chicago_IL/When_To_Visit/</u>

Chapter 5

16personalities.com <u>https://www.16personalities.com/</u>

Chapter 7

Forbes.com- https://www.forbes.com/advisor/mortgages/mortgage-to-income-ratio/#:~:text=The%2028%25%20rule%20says%20that,before%20taxes%20are%20taken%20out.

Made in the USA
Columbia, SC
09 October 2024

43335730R00072